skinny quilts and table runners

from today's top designers

edited by ELEANOR LEVIE

Martingale® & COMPANY

Skinny Quilts and Table Runners: From Today's Top Designers
© 2008 by Eleanor Levie

That Patchwork Place® is an imprint of Martingale
& Company®.

Martingale & Company
20205 144th Ave. NE
Woodinville, WA 98072-8478
www.martingale-pub.com

Printed in China
13 12 11 10 09 08   8 7 6 5 4 3 2 1

Library of Congress Cataloging-in-Publication Data
Library of Congress Control Number: 2007030963
ISBN: 978-1-56477-730-0

MISSION STATEMENT

Dedicated to providing quality products
and service to inspire creativity.

CREDITS

President & CEO: Tom Wierzbicki

Publisher: Jane Hamada

Editorial Director: Mary V. Green

Managing Editor: Tina Cook

Developmental Editor: Karen Costello Soltys

Technical Editor: Darra Williamson

Copy Editor: Melissa Bryan

Design Director: Stan Green

Assistant Design Director: Regina Girard

Illustrator: Robin Strobel

Cover & Text Designer: Shelly Garrison

Photographer: Brent Kane

Photo Stylists: Karen Clifton, Shelly
Garrison, Stan Green, Brent Kane, and
Karen Costello Soltys

DEDICATION

To Carl, my wonderful tall and skinny husband

ACKNOWLEDGMENTS

Big, fat thank-yous to

- The contributors—all stars of the quilting world—for sharing their considerable hearts and talents with me.

- Karen Soltys and Tina Cook, for their open and insightful minds that led the book through acquisition, development, and publication.

- Darra Williamson, for her great instincts regarding how-to text, and for her finely tuned ear for creative copy that sings.

- Photographer Brent Kane, photo stylist Karen Clifton, and designer Shelly Garrison, under the art direction of Stan Green, for their savvy eyes and exquisite sense of style.

- And everyone at Martingale & Company who lent a creative hand or provided more than a little legwork to make *Skinny Quilts and Table Runners* a reality.

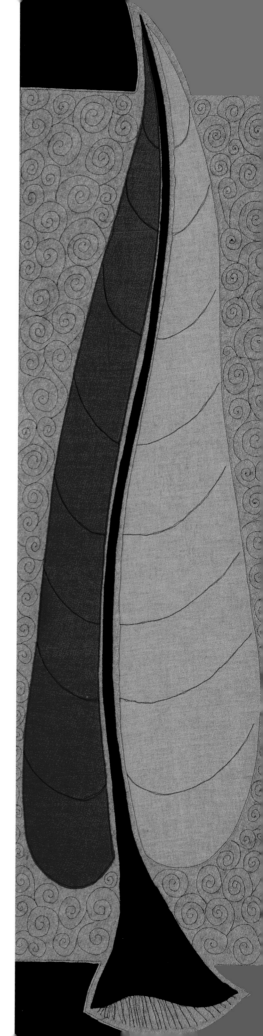

CONTENTS

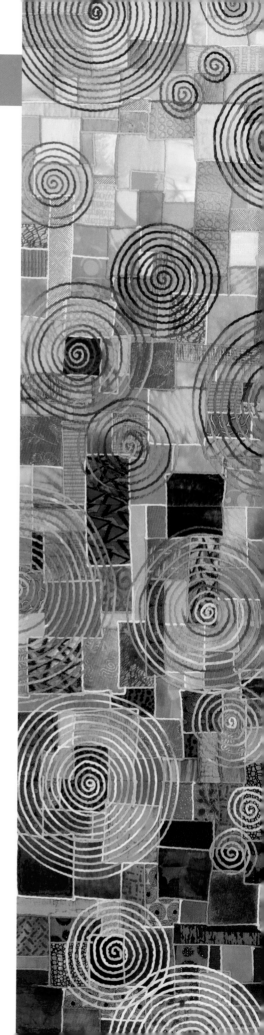

INTRODUCTION

You're loaded with taste, but low on time. You're dying to try a new technique, but without a big investment in fabric and supplies. You need the perfect gift, but nothing in the stores seems right. The solution? Make a "Skinny Quilt." Its long, narrow shape gives you an easy and unique opportunity for creativity; no other quilt is more versatile, as art or as craft.

A little background: My life is a crazy quilt. What with catering to my family ("the Jewish Martha Stewart" is a very demanding role), freelance editing, Sunday school teaching, way too many volunteer jobs—heck, it's downright hectic around here. I always need a gift in a hurry, and I *don't* wanna shop 'til I drop. Skinny Quilts to the rescue, whether I need something wonderful to dress my host's party table, a new look for an easy chair for my best friend's birthday, instant decor for my husband's new office, or a "traditional" gift for the appropriate anniversaries of family and friends. (Think cotton for the newlyweds celebrating two years of marriage, wool for that seven-year itch, and silk for the couple with a dozen years of wedded bliss under their belts.) Each gift is personalized in the recipients' favorite colors and customized to fit a particular table or space. I can't buy a better gift anywhere. And there are always fat paybacks: the way the recipients gush over the swanky, lanky creation (which took me just a few hours), you'd think I'd spent months—or even decades—on a queen-size quilt. The new owners love to show off their Skinny Quilts, placing them in the most public areas of their homes, unlike a quilt that's hidden away in the bedroom.

So the topic for this book was a no-brainer, and planning was a cinch. I simply asked my favorite quilters and fabric artists, all well-loved teachers and designers, to each create a Skinny Quilt that reflects their unique style. I was absolutely wowed by their response, and felt inspired to toss in a design of my own.

Whether you're a beginner or an experienced quilter; a piecer or a devotee of appliqué; take your quilt designs straight up, go for tradition with a twist, or submit to intoxicatingly arty adventures, this book has something for you. And just wait 'til your friends and family get a look at your masterpiece, finished in next to no time. No doubt about it—Skinny Quilts will bring you big fat rewards in the way of compliments!

—Eleanor Levie

Well-Adjusted Skinny Quilts—and Quiltmakers!

You know what you like. You've fallen in love with one of the designs in this book, and you're chomping at the bit to make it. But before you do, stop and take stock: Do you have a place in mind for this Skinny Quilt? Should you shorten the length to provide nice margins of table surface at both ends, or lengthen it for a generous overhang? Can you tailor the dimensions so it fits into the recessed panels of a door, or neatly covers the top of that upright piano? You get the picture. As long as you're making this quilt, you might as well optimize, maximize, improvise, and make it work for you. Ask at your local quilt shop if you need help refiguring the math or required fabric amounts, or choosing a good mix of fabric solids and prints.

Start with the fabrics that are absolutely perfect for the project and for the decor of its intended new home. A Skinny Quilt is obviously an economical project, because it doesn't require a lot of fabric, but this is no time to "make do." A Skinny Quilt isn't gonna help you deplete your stash anyway. Go buy those new fabrics right now, and splurge on top quality. You're worth it!

ROSY runner

*O*n a rare visit by Londoner Kaffe Fassett to the Pennsylvania home and studio of Liza Prior Lucy, the design partners decided to revisit a popular classic for this book. Like their very first "Rosy"-colored bed quilt and subsequent versions in other color palettes, this supremely simple Skinny Quilt alternates Nine Patch and plain blocks.

Quiltmakers accustomed to combining high-contrast light, medium, and dark fabrics may enjoy trying Kaffe and Liza's signature "low-contrast" look. In this rendition, the fabrics are mostly bright, and mostly designed by Kaffe (see "Resources" on page 91). Liza stresses that this is a scrap quilt, and encourages quiltmakers to *"place the fabrics any which way . . . it isn't possible to do it wrong!"*

By Kaffe Fassett and Liza Prior Lucy; machine quilted by Judy Irish

Finished measurements: 18½" x 72½"

MATERIALS

Yardages are based on fabrics that measure 42" wide.

1 yard *total* of assorted small- to medium-scale prints for Nine Patch blocks

⅔ yard *total* of assorted coordinating large-scale prints for plain squares

¼ yard of very large-scale floral print for plain squares*

½ yard of light dotted print for binding

2⅓ yards of fabric for backing

22" x 76" piece of cotton batting

Yardage may vary depending upon fabric repeat.

CUTTING

Cut all strips on the crosswise grain of the fabric (selvage to selvage) unless instructed otherwise.

From the assorted small- to medium-scale prints, cut a *total* of:
162 squares, 2½" x 2½"*

From the very large-scale floral, fussy cut:
4 squares, 6½" x 6½"**

From the assorted coordinating large-scale prints, cut a *total* of:
14 squares, 6½" x 6½"

From the dotted print, cut:
5 strips, 2¼" x 42"

From the *lengthwise grain* of the backing fabric, cut:
1 rectangle, 22" x 76"

*Cut these squares in 18 assorted sets of five matching squares and 18 assorted sets of four matching squares.

**Center the very large-scale floral motif in each square.

Cut Extras and Play!

Cut a few extra 6½" and 2½" squares to allow for optimum flexibility in arranging the fabrics and colors.

MAKING THE NINE PATCH BLOCKS

Arrange five matching 2½" small- or medium-scale print squares and four matching 2½" squares cut from a different small- or medium-scale print as shown. Strive for a pleasing balance of colors. Sew the squares into rows; press. Pin and stitch the rows together, carefully matching and nesting the seam allowances for accuracy; press. Make 18 blocks.

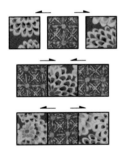 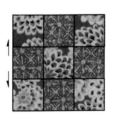

Make 18.

Be Unpredictable!

Here and there, replace one 2½" print square with one cut from another fabric. Such intentional "errors" add surprise and charm to your piece, and enable the prints and colors to blend better throughout the quilt.

ASSEMBLING THE QUILT TOP

Work on a large, flat surface such as a design wall, a table, or floor.

1. Arrange the 6½" fussy-cut squares, the 6½" large-scale print squares, and the Nine Patch blocks in 12 horizontal rows of three squares/blocks each, alternating them as shown in the assembly diagram below. Take time to rearrange the squares and blocks, scattering the fussy-cut blocks and colors evenly.

2. Sew the blocks together into rows; press.

3. Pin and sew the rows together, carefully matching the seam allowances for accuracy; press.

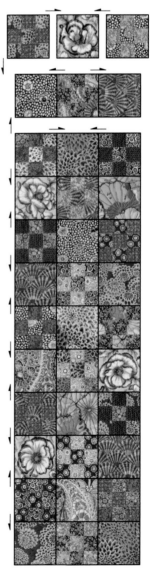

Assembly diagram

FINISHING

Refer to "Quiltmaking Basics" on page 87 as needed.

1. Press the quilt top. Layer the backing, batting, and quilt top; baste.

2. Quilt as desired or machine quilt in the ditch around all blocks and squares to anchor the layers. Free-motion quilt the 6½" squares following the pattern in each fabric to outline the large motifs. If desired, free-motion quilt a simple, continuous-line pattern on each patch of each Nine Patch block.

3. Trim the batting and backing even with the edges of the quilt top. Use the 2¼"-wide dotted-print strips to make and attach a double-fold binding.

Summer PICNIC

*O*rdinarily Laurie Shifrin looks to Mother Nature as her muse, but she reports that a bag of colorful plastic drinking straws in blues and greens generated the idea for this table runner. As with most of Laurie's designs, batiks provide rich colors and mottled or quiet patterning. Slender strips of folded fabric are inserted into the seams of the classic Rail Fence block, and although these strips are pressed flat, they certainly convey the original—and unusual—inspiration. Despite the on-point arrangement of blocks, the pieced inner border, and the free-hand, free-motion quilting pattern, this runner is a picnic to make. Try it to add a fresh, textural accent to your kitchen island or dining table.

By Laurie Shifrin

Finished measurements: 17⅞" x 51¾"

MATERIALS

Yardages are based on fabrics that measure 42" wide.

1¾ yards of lime-and-blue floral batik for setting triangles, outer border, and binding

⅜ yard *each* of lime green, blue, turquoise, and navy batik for blocks and pieced inner border

1¾ yards of fabric for backing

22" x 56" piece of batting

Medium blue or turquoise thread for machine quilting

CUTTING

Cut all strips on the crosswise grain of the fabric (selvage to selvage) unless instructed otherwise.

From *each* lime green, blue, turquoise, and navy batik, cut:
3 strips, 1" x 42" (12 total)

4 strips, 1½" x 42" (16 total)

From the remaining yardage of the lime green, blue, turquoise, and navy batiks, cut a *total* of:
3 strips, 1" x 20"

3 strips, 1½" x 20"

From the *lengthwise grain* of the lime-and-blue floral batik, cut:
3 strips, 2¾" x 56"

3 strips, 2¼" x 56"

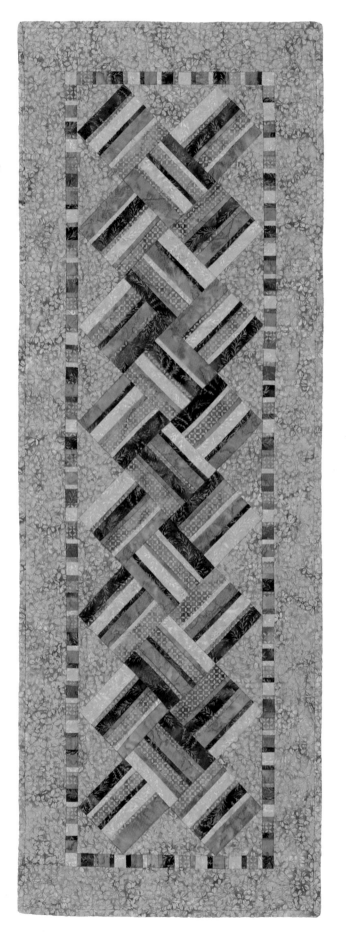

From the remaining lime-and-blue floral batik, cut:

4 squares, 7" x 7"; cut each square in half twice diagonally to yield 16 quarter-square triangles

2 squares, 3¾" x 3¾"; cut each square in half once diagonally to yield 4 half-square triangles

From the *lengthwise grain* of the backing fabric, cut:

1 rectangle, 22" x 56", for binding

MAKING THE BLOCKS

1. Fold each 1" x 42" lime green, blue, turquoise, and navy strip in half lengthwise; press. (With batik fabric, there's no need to worry about folding with a certain side facing out—both sides are the right side!) Make 12.

2. Align the raw edges of a folded strip along the long edge of a 1½" x 42" different-colored batik strip. Machine baste the two strips together with a ³/₁₆" seam allowance as shown. Make 12 scrappy combinations, three using each color of the 1½" x 42" strips. Press the seam allowances flat.

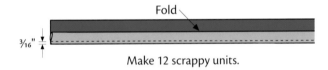

Make 12 scrappy units.

3. Cut each unit from step 2 and each remaining 1½" x 42" batik strip in half crosswise to yield two 1½" x 20" units/strips. Sort the units and strips into eight groups of three scrappy units and one contrasting 1½"-wide batik strip.

4. Reset your sewing machine to a regular stitch length (10 to 12 stitches per inch). Working one group at a time, arrange and sew the three units and one batik strip together along their long edges to make a flanged strip set as shown. Press, taking care to keep the folded edges flat and smooth. Make eight strip sets. Crosscut each strip set into three 4½" blocks (24 total). Set the remaining portions aside for the pieced inner border.

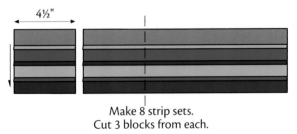

4½"

Make 8 strip sets.
Cut 3 blocks from each.

ASSEMBLING THE QUILT TOP

Work on a large, flat surface such as a design wall, a table, or floor.

1. Arrange the blocks, the floral quarter-square side setting triangles, and the floral half-square corner setting triangles in diagonal rows, alternating the orientation of the strips (horizontal versus vertical) as shown in the assembly diagram. Rearrange the blocks as necessary to achieve a pleasing color balance. You will have one block left over; set this aside for another project.

2. Sew the blocks and side setting triangles together in diagonal rows. Press, taking care to keep the folded edges smooth and flat.

3. Pin and then sew the rows together, carefully matching the seam allowances for accuracy. Add the corner setting triangles; press.

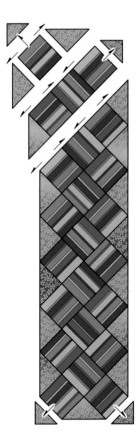

Assembly diagram

ADDING THE BORDERS

1. Use the three 1" x 20" batik strips and the three 1½" x 20" batik strips to make a strip set with folded inserts as described in "Making the Blocks" on page 14. Note that this strip set does not include the extra 1½"-wide batik strip.

2. Use a seam ripper to remove the plain 1½"-wide batik strip from each remaining strip-set segment from "Making the Blocks." Crosscut the strip set you made in step 1 and these strip-set segments into a total of 40 segments, 1¼" wide. Stitch the segments together end to end in random order to make one long pieced strip. Make sure all the folded inserts face in the same direction.

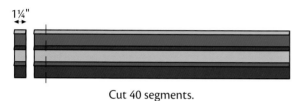

1¼"

Cut 40 segments.

3. Measure the length of the quilt top through the center. Use a seam ripper to remove a portion of the long pieced strip equal to this measurement, adjusting as necessary to avoid having the ends of the new strip fall on a folded insert. Make two. Pin and sew one pieced strip to each long side of the quilt top. Press the seam allowances toward the center of the quilt top.

4. Measure the width of the quilt top through the center, including the borders just added. Repeat step 3 to separate, pin, and sew a pieced border strip to the top and bottom of the quilt top; press.

5. Measure the length of the quilt through the center. Trim two 2¾"-wide floral outer-border strips to this length. Pin and sew one strip to each long side of the quilt. Press the seam allowances toward the newly added border.

6. Measure the width of the quilt through the center, including the borders just added. Repeat step 5 to trim, pin, and sew a 2¾"-wide floral outer-border strip to the top and bottom of the quilt top; press.

No Binding Measures

Simulate the look of binding that matches the borders and backing. Either topstitch over an envelope finish or fold the edges of the backing over the quilt top.

FINISHING

Refer to "Quiltmaking Basics" on page 87 as needed.

1. Press the quilt top. Layer the backing, batting, and quilt top; baste.

2. Quilt as desired or machine quilt in the ditch around each block and along the pieced inner border, and then use turquoise or blue thread to free-motion quilt a simple posy design in each setting triangle and in the outer border.

3. Trim the batting and backing even with the edges of the quilt top. Use the 2¼"-wide floral strips to make and attach a double-fold binding.

Pinwheels

Terry is rightfully proud "to make simple quilts that look like they are more work than they really are." This Pinwheel pattern, loosely based on the easiest of blocks, the Courthouse Steps version of the traditional Log Cabin, is a case in point—or rather, on point. The new "spin" is a welcome change from the typical Pinwheel that requires matching eight seams in the center of the block. With this Pinwheel, there are no center seams whatsoever to match. Fabric logs compose and frame the block, build the setting triangles, and cap the pointed ends. When made with a bunch of fat quarters and fat eighths in fresh prints, these Pinwheels are a breeze!

By Terry Atkinson of Atkinson Designs

Finished measurements: 15⅛" x 52⅛"

MATERIALS

Yardages are based on fabric that measures 42" wide. Fat quarters measure 18" x 21". Fat eighths measure 9" x 21".

Fat quarter *each* of 8 assorted colorful prints for blocks, setting triangles, and binding

Fat quarter of light-on-white print for blocks

Fat eighth of yellow print for blocks

⅞ yard of fabric for backing

19" x 56" piece of thin batting

CUTTING

Cut all strips on the crosswise grain of the fabric (selvage to selvage).

From *each* of 3 assorted colorful prints, cut:
1 strip, 1¾" x 21"; crosscut into:

    2 rectangles, 1¾" x 4½" (6 total)

    2 rectangles, 1¾" x 2" (6 total)

4 squares, 2½" x 2½" (12 total)

From the yellow print, cut:
3 squares, 2" x 2"

1 square, 3½" x 3½"; cut in half twice diagonally to yield
    4 quarter-square triangles

From the light-on-white print, cut:
5 strips, 2½" x 21"; crosscut into:

    12 rectangles, 2½" x 4½"

    12 squares, 2½" x 2½"

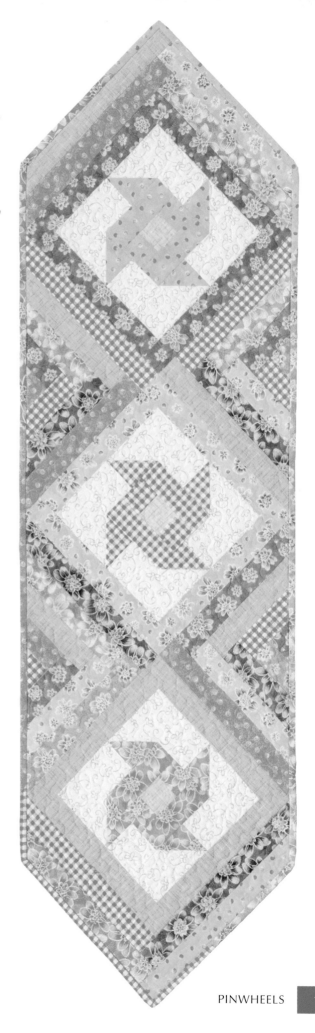

From *each* of 3 remaining colorful prints, cut:

2 strips, 1¾" x 21" (6 total); crosscut *each* strip into:

  1 strip, 1¾" x 8½" (6 total)

  1 strip, 1¾" x 11" (6 total)

From the remaining yardage of the 8 colorful prints, cut a *total* of:*

24 strips, 1¾" x 21"; crosscut into:

  8 strips, 1¾" x 12" (H)

  8 strips, 1¾" x 11" (G)

  4 strips, 1¾" x 9½" (F)

  4 strips, 1¾" x 8½" (E)

  4 strips, 1¾" x 7" (D)

  4 strips, 1¾" x 6" (C)

  4 strips, 1¾" x 4½" (B)

  4 strips, 1¾" x 3½" (A)

8 strips, 2¼" x 21"

Cutting the longer pieces first ensures you will have enough fabric.

MAKING THE PINWHEEL BLOCKS

1. Stitch matching 1¾" x 2" colorful print rectangles to the top and bottom edges of a 2" yellow square; press. Stitch 1¾" x 4½" rectangles in the same print to the sides; press.

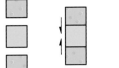

2. Use a pencil to mark a diagonal line on the wrong side of four matching 2½" colorful print squares. With right sides together and raw edges aligned, place a marked square on a 2½" light-on-white square. Stitch directly on the marked line. Trim ¼" beyond the stitching line; press. Make two.

3. Sew a 2½" light-on-white square to each unit from step 2, taking care to orient the unit as shown; press. Make two.

Make 2.

4. Place a remaining marked 2½" colorful print square on the corner of a 2½" x 4½" light-on-white rectangle. Stitch, trim, and press. Make two.

Stitch.   Trim.   Press.

5. Sew a 2½" x 4½" light-on-white rectangle and a unit from step 4 together as shown; press. Make two.

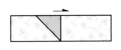

Make 2.

6. Sew a unit from step 3 to the top and bottom of the unit from step 1 as shown; press. Sew units from step 5 to the sides; press.

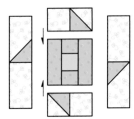 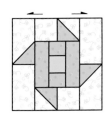

7. Sew matching 1¾" x 8½" strips of one of three colorful prints to the top and bottom of the unit from step 6; press. Sew 1¾" x 11" strips in the same print to the sides; press.

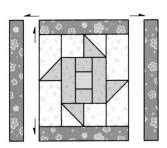

8. Repeat steps 1–7 to make a total of three Pinwheel blocks, each using different-colored prints.

MAKING THE LOG CABIN SETTING TRIANGLES

You will use the 1¾"-wide assorted colorful strips in varying lengths (strips A–H) to make the Log Cabin setting triangles. Refer to the quilt photo on page 17 as needed.

1. Sew an A strip to one short side of a yellow quarter-square triangle; press. Sew a B strip to the adjacent short side of the unit; press. Add strips C, D, E, F, G, and H, alternating the same two sides of the quarter-square triangle as shown. Press the seams toward each newly added strip as you go, and then apply spray starch and press the finished unit.

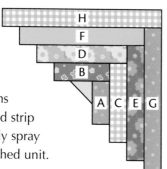

2. Use a ruler and a pencil to measure 11⅞" from the 90° corner of the step 1 unit along both adjacent edges. Draw a diagonal line connecting the two points. Stay stitch ¼" *inside* the drawn line, and then trim directly on the drawn line.

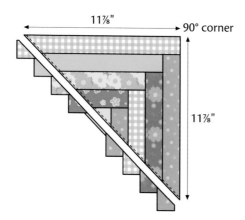

11⅞"   90° corner

11⅞"

Stay stitch and trim.

3. Repeat steps 1 and 2 to make a total of four setting triangles. Set the remaining G and H strips aside for now. You will use them later to complete the quilt top.

ASSEMBLING THE QUILT TOP

Work on a large, flat surface such as a design wall, a table, or floor.

1. Arrange the Pinwheel blocks and setting triangles as shown in the assembly diagram.

2. Sew two remaining G and H strips to two sides of the top and bottom Pinwheel blocks, alternating G, H, G,

and H as shown. Press the seam allowances toward each newly added strip as you go.

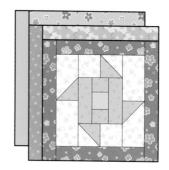

3. Sew the blocks and setting triangles together in diagonal rows as shown; press.

4. Sew the rows together; press. Trim the corners of the top and bottom Pinwheel blocks even with the sides of the quilt top.

FINISHING

Refer to "Quiltmaking Basics" on page 87 as needed.

1. Divide the backing fabric in half lengthwise. Remove the selvages and, with right sides together, pin the halves together along the short edges; sew and press.

2. Press the quilt top. Layer the backing, batting, and quilt top; baste.

3. Quilt as desired or free-motion quilt the center of each Pinwheel with a spiral, leaving the rest of the print areas of the block free of quilting. Quilt the background of each block with a loop-de-loop motif, and the setting triangles and strips in an overall meander pattern.

4. Trim the batting and backing even with the edges of the quilt top. Use the 2¼"-wide colorful print strips to make and attach a double-fold binding.

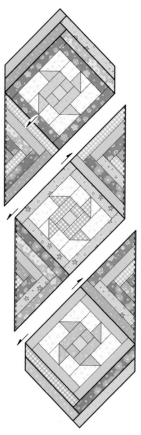

Assembly diagram

Darlene Zimmerman, aka "The Feedsack Lady," specializes in collecting and reproducing 1930s-style fabrics as well as creating new quilt classics. Darlene has also designed many popular quilting tools, and she preaches precision and speed with a variety of quick-cutting and quick-piecing techniques.

This light, fresh version of the Evening Star pattern features Darlene's feedsack reproduction prints in various pastels (see "Resources" on page 91), but you can use fabrics that complement your decor and make the proper number of Evening Star blocks and setting triangles to fit your table.

By Darlene Zimmerman

Finished measurements: 17¾" x 68", including prairie points

MATERIALS

Yardages are based on fabrics that measure 42" wide. Fat quarters measure 18" x 21".

¾ yard of white solid or tone-on-tone print for blocks and setting triangles

⅜ yard of pastel print for border

Fat quarter *each* of 5 assorted pastel prints for blocks, setting triangles, and prairie points

1¼ yards of fabric for backing

20" x 72" piece of batting

Small piece of template material

CUTTING

Cut all strips on the crosswise grain of the fabric (selvage to selvage) unless instructed otherwise. Use the full-size patterns on page 25 to make templates for A and B. If you prefer, you can use Darlene's Tri-Recs and Companion Angle acrylic triangle templates to cut pieces A and B (see "Resources" on page 91). Refer to the product packaging for guidance.

From *each* pastel print fat quarter, cut:
1 strip, 3½" x 21", cut into:

    1 square, 3½" x 3½" (5 total)

    4 B triangles and 4 B reverse (40 total; 20 and 20 reverse)

2 strips, 2" x 21" (10 total)

2 strips, 3" x 21"; crosscut into 14 squares, 3" x 3" (70 total)

From the white solid or tone-on-tone print, cut:

6 squares, 6" x 6"; cut each square in half twice diagonally to yield 24 quarter-square triangles

2 strips, 3½" x 42"; cut into 20 A triangles

5 strips, 2" x 42"; crosscut in half to yield 10 strips, 2" x 21"

From the pastel print for border, cut:

5 strips, 2" x 42"

ASSEMBLING THE EVENING STAR BLOCKS

1. With right sides together, sew a pastel B triangle to a white A triangle, matching the blunted point of the A triangle with the bottom of the B triangle as shown; press. Repeat to sew a matching B reverse triangle to the opposite side of the unit. Make 20 in matching sets of four.

Make 20.

2. With right sides together, sew a 2" x 21" white strip and a 2" x 21" pastel strip together along their long edges to make a strip set as shown; press. Make 10 scrappy strip sets. Cut the strip sets into 90 segments, 2" wide.

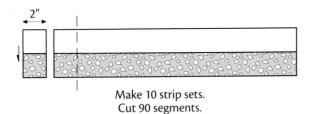

Make 10 strip sets.
Cut 90 segments.

3. Arrange and sew two scrappy segments from step 2 together to make a four-patch unit as shown; press. Make 45.

Make 45.

4. Arrange four matching units from step 1, a matching 3½" print square, and four scrappy units from step 3, taking extra care to position the step 3 units as shown. Sew the units and squares into rows; press. Sew the rows together; press. Make five blocks.

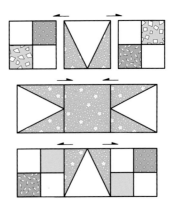

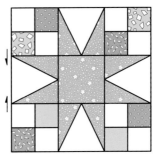

Make 5.

MAKING THE SETTING TRIANGLES

Arrange three remaining scrappy four-patch units and three white quarter-square triangles, taking care to position the four-patch units as shown. Sew the units and triangles into rows; press. Sew the rows together; press. Make eight. You will have one four-patch unit left over; set this aside for another project.

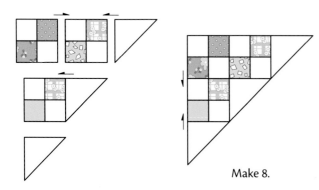

Make 8.

ASSEMBLING THE QUILT TOP

Work on a large, flat surface such as a design wall, a table, or floor.

1. Arrange the blocks and setting triangles as shown in the assembly diagram.

2. Sew the blocks and setting triangles together into diagonal rows as shown; press.

3. Sew the rows together; press.

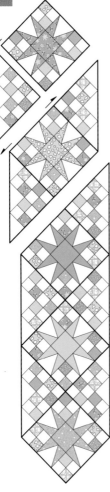

Assembly diagram

4. Use a rotary cutter and ruler to trim and straighten the long edges of the quilt top, making sure to leave a ¼" seam allowance from the corners of the four-patch units in the blocks and setting triangles.

ADDING THE BORDERS

1. Sew the 2" x 42" pastel strips together with diagonal seams to make one long strip. Press the seam allowances open. From this strip, cut two borders, 2" x 55".

2. With right sides together and matching center points, pin and sew a 2" x 55" pastel strip to each long edge of the quilt top; press. Trim the ends of the strips following the angle of the quilt top.

Trim.

3. Sew the remaining length of 2"-wide pastel strip to the left edge of one pointed end of the quilt top; press. Trim the ends of the strip even with the quilt top. Repeat to sew the remaining length of the print strip to the right edge of the point; press and trim.

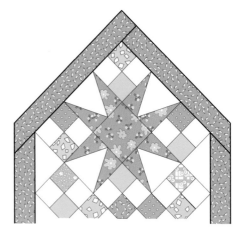

4. Repeat step 3 to sew the remaining length of the print strip to both sides of the opposite pointed end of the quilt top.

ADDING THE PRAIRIE POINTS

1. Fold each 3" assorted print square in half once on the diagonal; press. Fold again as shown; press. Make 68. You will have two squares left over; set these aside for another project.

Make 68.

2. Beginning at one pointed end of the quilt top, align and pin the raw edges of the prairie points with the raw edges of the quilt top so the tips of the prairie points face inward and the open edges all face the same direction. Tuck the folded edge of each prairie point inside the open edges of the adjacent prairie point. Place 5 prairie points on each short pointed side of the quilt top and 24 prairie points on each long side.

3. Stitch the prairie points to the quilt with a ¼" seam allowance.

FINISHING

Refer to "Quiltmaking Basics" on page 87 as needed.

1. Divide the backing fabric in half lengthwise. Remove the selvages and, with right sides together, pin the halves together along the short edges; sew and press. Trim the backing to measure 20" x 72".

2. Press the quilt top. Layer the backing, batting, and quilt top; baste.

3. Quilt as desired or machine quilt in the ditch around all the shapes cut from printed fabrics and in a small-scale meandering motif in the white background areas. Hand or machine quilt a square-in-a-square design in the center of each Evening Star block. Leave the border area free from quilting.

4. Trim the backing and batting even with the edge of the quilt top. Fold and pin the quilt top and backing out of the way, and trim ¼" from the batting only. Fold the raw edges of the quilt top and prairie points over the edges of the batting, and then fold the raw edges of the backing ¼" to the wrong side and pin them to the quilt top so that the folded edges are flush and the stitching line attaching the prairie points is covered. Slip-stitch the folded edge of the backing to the prairie points, trimming the excess fabric at the corners as needed.

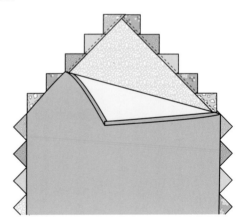

5. Quilt the border as desired. The border of the quilt shown was free-motion machine quilted with a continuous-line spiral pattern.

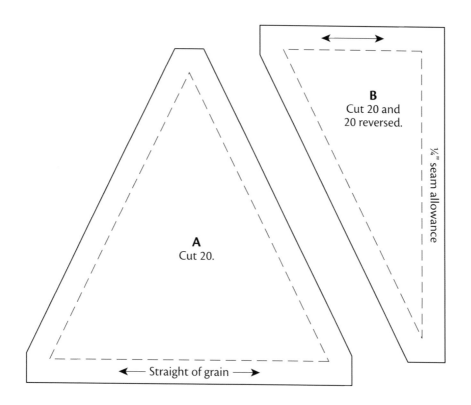

A
Cut 20.

← Straight of grain →

B
Cut 20 and
20 reversed.

¼" seam allowance

Astrological

Marti Michell has long promoted what she loves in quilts: 100%-cotton fabrics and Log Cabin designs. Her creative energy is going strong—she has recently created yet another, new and better way to build this classic block. Strips (or "logs") are rotary cut as usual, but along the least-stretchy, lengthwise grain. In addition, they are cut to the exact lengths needed, a process made even easier with Marti's new Log Cabin rulers (see "Resources" on page 91).

Regardless of the rotary tools you use, the work is more efficient, the results are more precise, and multiple blocks are far more consistent in size. Construction is as easy as, well, falling off a log. Add a brilliant sashing of Compass Stars and Evening Stars, and—oh my stars!—the blocks practically disappear into a galaxy on your table.

By Marti Michell

Finished measurements: 15" x 43⅞"

MATERIALS

Yardages are based on fabrics that measure 42" wide. Fat quarters measure 18" x 21". Fat eighths measure 9" x 21".

½ yard of black small-scale print for blocks, sashing strips, and binding

½ yard of black medium-scale print for sashing strips and setting triangles

Fat quarter *each* of 6 assorted white small-scale prints for blocks and sashing strips

Fat quarter *each* of 7 additional assorted black small-scale prints for blocks and sashing strips

¼ yard of hot pink fabric for blocks, sashing strips, small setting triangles, and flat piping (insets)

Fat eighth of orange fabric for sashing, sashing corner squares, and small setting triangles

1½ yards of fabric for backing

19" x 48" piece of batting

Clear monofilament for quilting

CUTTING

Cut all strips on the crosswise grain of the fabric (selvage to selvage) unless instructed otherwise. If you wish, fussy cut any fabric that has a special design, such as lines of text or bars of music.

From the *lengthwise grain* (18" edge) of the fat quarters of white small-scale prints, cut a *total* of:

18 strips, 1¼" x 18"*

From the *lengthwise grain* (18" edge) of the fat quarters of black small-scale prints, cut a *total* of:

29 strips, 1¼" x 18"*

From the *lengthwise grain* of the ½ yard of black small-scale print, cut:

1 strip, 1¼" x 18"

From the remaining ½ yard of black small-scale print, cut:

4 strips, 2¼" x 36"

From the black medium-scale print, cut:

3 squares, 9" x 9"; cut each square in half twice diagonally to yield 12 quarter-square triangles. You will have 2 triangles left over; set them aside for another project.

1 square, 4¾" x 4¾"; cut it in half once diagonally to yield 2 half-square triangles

2 strips, 2" x 7"

From the hot pink fabric, cut:

2 strips, 1¼" x 42"; crosscut into 56 squares, 1¼" x 1¼"

1 square, 2⅜" x 2⅜"; cut in half once diagonally to yield 2 half-square triangles

1 strip, 2" x 16"; crosscut into 8 squares, 2" x 2"

2 squares, 2¾" x 2¾"; cut each square in half twice diagonally to yield 8 quarter-square triangles. You will have 3 triangles left over; set them aside for another project.

3 strips, ⅞" x 42"

From the orange fabric, cut:

1 square, 2⅜" x 2⅜"; cut in half once diagonally to yield 2 half-square triangles

1 strip, 2" x 21"; crosscut into 8 squares, 2" x 2"

2 squares, 2¾" x 2¾"; cut each square in half twice diagonally to yield 8 quarter-square triangles. You will have 3 triangles left over; set them aside for another project.

From the *lengthwise grain* of the backing fabric, cut:

1 piece, 19" x 48"

You are cutting a few extra strips to give you additional variety in creating the scrappy blocks.

ASSEMBLING THE BLOCKS

You will use two variations of the traditional Log Cabin block for this quilt: six of block 1 and two of block 2. Chain piece as described for maximum efficiency. Finger-press the seams outward from the block center as you go, and grade the seam allowances to prevent fabrics from shadowing through the white fabric. Press with a hot, dry iron periodically as instructed.

1. Shuffle and stack the 1¼"-wide white strips in one stack and the 1¼"-wide black small-scale strips in another. Crosscut the strips into the following lengths, beginning with the longest lengths (G) and proceeding to the shortest (A). Cut up to four layers at a time, and use labels or sticky notes to identify the strips by letter. Cut a total of:

    44 black strips and 14 white strips, 1¼" x 5¾" (G)

    8 black strips and 8 white strips, 1¼" x 5" (F)

    10 black strips and 6 white strips, 1¼" x 4¼" (E)

    8 black strips and 8 white strips, 1¼" x 3½" (D)

    10 black strips and 6 white strips, 1¼" x 2¾" (C)

    8 black strips and 8 white strips, 1¼" x 2" (B)

    2 black squares and 6 white squares, 1¼" x 1¼" (A)

2. Place six 1¼" pink squares to the left of your sewing machine. Arrange the white squares and strips and the black squares and strips you cut in step 1 in parallel stacks in alphabetical order to the left of the pink squares as shown. The A strips should be closest to you and the G strips farthest away.

3. With right sides together and raw edges aligned, sew a white A square to a 1¼" pink square. Make six using the chain-piecing technique shown. Cut the chain-pieced units apart; finger-press.

Make 6.

4. Place each unit from step 3 right sides together with a white B strip. Chain piece, making sure to lead with the pink square. Make six.

5. Referring to the diagram below and working clockwise, continue to add 1¼"-wide white and black strips in alphabetical order around the block center. Use a hot, dry iron to press well after adding the C strips, and then again after adding each full round of strips around the block center. Make six scrappy blocks and label them block 1.

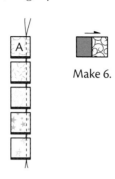

Block 1.
Make 6.

Seams to Be Your Guide

Starting with the C strips, it's easy to stay on track. Just place each new strip along an edge with two seams.

6. Follow steps 3–5 to make two blocks, placing the 1¼"-wide white and black strips as shown. Label them block 2. You will have some black and white G strips left over; you will use them to make the sashing units.

Block 2.
Make 2.

MAKING THE SASHING UNITS

1. Sew two scrappy black G strips together along their long edges; press. Make six.

Make 6.

2. Sew a unit from step 1 between a pink half-square triangle and an orange half-square triangle as shown; press. Make one of each and label them sashing unit a.

Sashing unit a.
Make 1 of each.

3. Use a pencil to mark a diagonal line on the wrong side of a 2" pink square. With right sides together and raw edges aligned, place a marked square on one end of a remaining unit from step 1. Stitch a hair's width outside the marked line. Trim ¼" beyond the stitching line; press. Make four and label them sashing unit b.

Sashing unit b.
Make 4.

4. Repeat step 3, substituting a 1¼" pink square for the 2" pink square and a single black G strip for the unit from step 1 as shown. Make 12 of each. Sew one of each unit together along their long edges; press. Make 12 and label them sashing unit c.

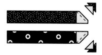

Sashing unit c.
Make 12.

5. Repeat step 3, substituting a 1¼" pink square for the 2" pink square and a single white G strip for the unit from step 1 as shown. Make four of each. Sew one of each unit together along their long edges; press. Make four.

Make 4.

6. Use the method described in step 3 to sew a 2" pink square to each unit from step 5. Make four and label them sashing unit d.

Sashing unit d.
Make 4.

7. Use the method described in step 3 to align and sew a 1¼" pink square to the upper-left corner of a 2" x 7" black medium-scale rectangle as shown. Press and trim. Sew a 1¼" pink square to the lower-left corner of the unit. Press and trim. Make two and label them sashing unit e.

Sashing unit e.
Make 2.

8. Use the method described in step 3 to sew a 1¼" pink square to opposite ends of a white G strip as shown; press. Make six. Sew two units together along their long edges; press. Make three and label them sashing unit f.

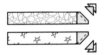

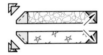

Sashing unit f.
Make 3.

ASSEMBLING THE QUILT TOP

Work on a large, flat surface such as a design wall, a table, or floor.

1. Arrange the blocks, the sashing units, the 2" orange squares, the black medium-scale quarter-square and half-square setting triangles, and the pink and orange quarter-square setting triangles in diagonal rows as shown in the assembly diagram.

2. Sew the blocks, sashing units, squares, quarter-square triangles, and half-square triangles together into diagonal rows as shown; press.

3. Sew the rows together; press.

Assembly diagram

4. Use a rotary cutter and ruler to straighten the long edges of the quilt top, making sure to leave a ¼" seam allowance all around. Square the corners.

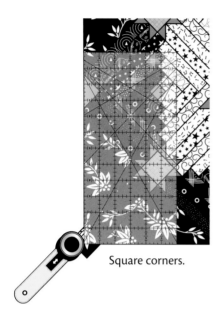

Square corners.

FINISHING

Refer to "Quiltmaking Basics" on page 87 as needed.

1. Press the quilt top. Layer the backing, batting, and quilt top; baste.

2. Quilt as desired or use clear monofilament to machine quilt in the ditch on the diagonal seams running in both directions between the blocks and sashing units.

3. Trim the batting and backing even with the edge of the quilt top.

4. For flat piping (insets), sew the ⅞" x 42" pink strips together with diagonal seams. Press the seam allowances open. Fold the strip in half lengthwise, with right sides out; press.

5. Measure the length of the quilt through the center and cut two folded pink strips to that measurement. Measure the width of the quilt through the center and cut two folded pink strips to that measurement.

6. Align the raw edges of one long folded strip to the raw edge on a long side of the quilt top. Stay stitch the strip in place using a ³/₁₆" seam. Repeat to baste the remaining long folded strip to the opposite side and the short folded strips to the top and bottom of the quilt.

7. Use the 2¼"-wide black strips to make and attach a double-fold binding.

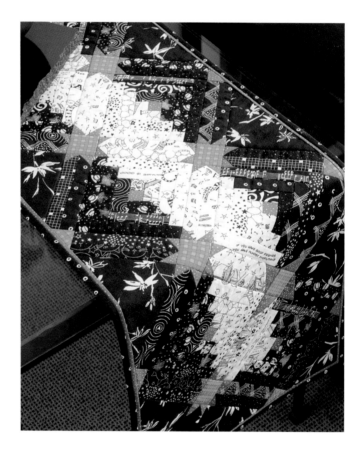

Churn DASH Stretch

Ready for a "skinny" version of a traditional block? Avis Shirer was inspired by this quilt assignment to stretch her imagination and the Churn Dash block, too. True to her usual primitive folk-art style, she rendered the repeat block design in a warm color palette and added simple wreaths of berry clusters. Pick up her cue and dash through this easy blending of patchwork and appliqué. After you lay the groundwork, Avis advises layering on wool embellishments, secured with just a dash of embroidery. "It gives a project so much texture," she raves.

By Avis Shirer of Joined at the Hip

Finished measurements: 15" x 52½"

MATERIALS

Yardages are based on fabric that measures 42" wide.

½ yard of tan print for block backgrounds

½ yard of blue print for blocks

½ yard of brown-and-black stripe for spacer bars and binding

½ yard of medium brown solid for border

¼ yard of chestnut brown small-scale print for wreath appliqués

Scraps of rust and olive felted wool for berry and leaf appliqués*

1¾ yards of fabric for backing

19" x 57" piece of cotton batting

½ yard of 18"-wide fusible web

Brown and tan threads for machine appliqué and quilting

Blue, orange, and green variegated threads for machine quilting and embroidery

See page 34 for instructions for making felted wool.

CUTTING

Cut all strips on the crosswise grain of the fabric (selvage to selvage) unless instructed otherwise.

From the tan print, cut:
6 squares, 3⅞" x 3⅞"

6 squares, 2½" x 2½"

9 rectangles, 2½" x 9½"

From the blue print, cut:
6 squares, 3⅞" x 3⅞"

6 rectangles, 1½" x 2½"

6 rectangles, 1½" x 9½"

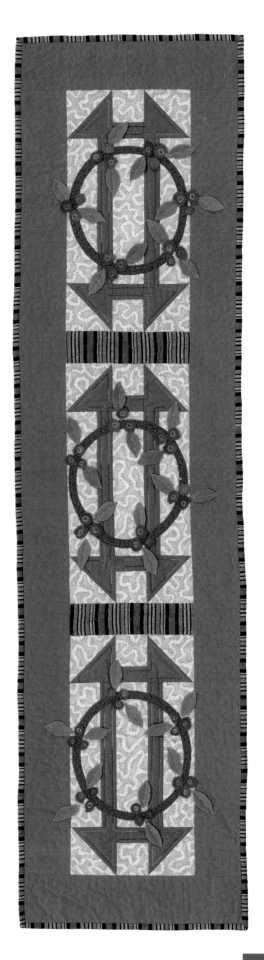

From the brown-and-black stripe, cut:

2 rectangles, 2½" x 8½"

4 strips, 2¼" x 42"

From the medium brown solid, cut:

4 strips, 3½" x 42"

From the _lengthwise grain_ of the backing fabric, cut:

1 piece, 19" x 57"

Do-It-Yourself Felting

The term _felting_ simply means washing wool fabric that's woven or knitted so that all the fibers shrink and meld together. Other terms for this process are shrinking or fulling the wool, or creating _boiled wool_—though it's not really necessary to use boiling water! Felted wool is a whole other ball of wax from most commercial felt, which is nonwoven, has its fibers pressed together under extreme pressure, and is rarely more than 35% wool.

Use 100% wool for the best felting results. Remove the selvage from wool yardage purchased off the bolt; this tightly woven edge does not shrink as much and will ruffle the fabric. If you are using wool cut from old garments—woven or knitted—rip apart or cut away the seams.

1. Fill your top-loading washing machine with hot water. If you have a front-loading washing machine, you won't get the best agitating process. In this case, take your wool to your neighbors' house and use their machine!

2. Put in the wool and agitate it on the heavy-duty or regular setting, using the longest cycle. The longer the agitation, the tighter your weave will become—and this is a good thing! The combination of the hot water and the agitation is what shrinks and felts your wool.

3. Rinse the wool in cold water and put it in the dryer on the regular, heat-dry setting. When the wool is completely dry, take it out and lay it flat.

4. Don't iron your felted wool. The iron will leave a sheen and flatten the soft nap. If the wool has fold lines or wrinkles, simply wet it and toss it in the dryer.

If you ever need to clean a Skinny Quilt made with felted wool, either have it dry-cleaned or wash it by hand in the bathtub using lukewarm water and a detergent that's designated for wool. Do not put the quilt in a washing machine and agitate it. Even though the wool has been prefelted, the agitation could shrink it again and distort the overall effect.

MAKING THE CHURN DASH BLOCKS

1. Use a pencil to mark a diagonal line on the wrong side of each 3⅞" tan square. With right sides together and raw edges aligned, place a marked square on a 3⅞" blue square. Make six. Stitch a scant ¼" from both sides of the line. Cut on the line to separate the sewn units; press. Make 12 half-square-triangle units.

Make 6.

Make 12.

2. Sew a 2½" tan square and a 1½" x 2½" blue rectangle together as shown; press. Make six.

Make 6.

3. Sew a 2½" x 9½" tan rectangle and a 1½" x 9½" blue rectangle together as shown; press. Make six.

Make 6.

4. Arrange the units from steps 1–3 and a remaining 2½" x 9½" tan rectangle as shown. Sew the units and rectangle together into rows; press. Sew the rows together; press. Make three blocks.

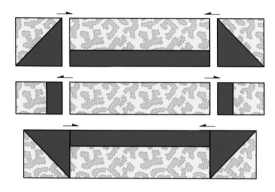

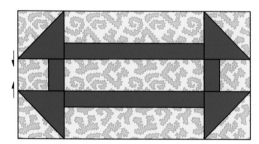

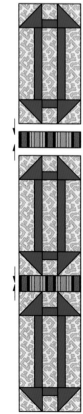

Make 3.

ASSEMBLING THE QUILT TOP

Work on a large, flat surface such as a design wall, a table, or floor.

1. Arrange the blocks and the 2½" x 8½" striped rectangles to make a vertical row, alternating them as shown in the assembly diagram. Sew the blocks and spacer bars together; press.

2. Sew the 3½"-wide brown border strips end to end with diagonal seams to make one long strip. Measure the length of the quilt top through the center. Cut two border strips to this measurement. Pin and sew one strip to each long side of the quilt. Press the seam allowances toward the border.

3. Measure the width of the quilt through the center, including the borders just added. Repeat step 2 to trim, pin, and sew a border strip to the top and bottom edges of the quilt top; press.

Assembly diagram

LAYERING AND QUILTING

Refer to "Quiltmaking Basics" on page 87 as needed.

1. Press the quilt top. Layer the backing, batting, and quilt top; baste.

2. Quilt as desired or machine quilt in the ditch around each shape in the Churn Dash blocks and in the seams between the spacer bars and border with tan thread. Quilt a diagonal lattice in each striped spacer bar. Use variegated blue thread to outline quilt ¼" from the seams around each blue piece in the Churn Dash blocks and tan thread to free-motion quilt a small meander pattern over the background patches on each block. Finish by quilting a larger meander pattern over the border with tan thread.

ADDING THE WREATHS, LEAVES, AND BERRIES

Refer to "Fusible Appliqué the Easy Way" on page 88 as needed.

1. Cut fusible web into three squares, 8½" x 8½". Fold each square horizontally and vertically into quarters with the paper side facing outward.

2. Use the quarter-wreath pattern on page 36 to make a template. Place the template on the paper side of the folded fusible web with the dashed lines along the folds; trace with a pencil or a fine-tip permanent marker. Roughly cut out along the marked lines and unfold. Referring to the manufacturer's instructions for the fusible web, fuse web to the brown print and cut out on the marked lines. Make three wreaths.

3. Referring to the quilt photo on page 33, center a prepared wreath on each Churn Dash block. Fuse the wreath in place. Finish the edges, inside and out, with brown thread and a buttonhole stitch.

4. Using the leaf pattern on page 36 as a guide, freehand-cut 36 leaves from the green felted wool. Use pinking shears to freehand-cut 54 berries, each approximately ⅝" in diameter, from the rust felted wool. (If you prefer, use the patterns to make templates.)

5. Referring to the quilt photo on page 33, arrange 18 berries and 12 leaves on each wreath; pin. Free-motion stitch a ¼" coil of orange variegated thread at the center of each berry. Use variegated green thread and a long stitch to sew a vein lengthwise down the center of each leaf.

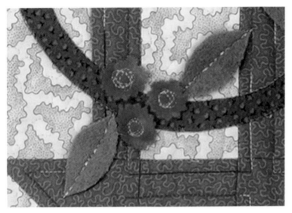

The edges of the leaves and berries are left free for added texture.

FINISHING

Refer to "Quiltmaking Basics" on page 87 as needed.

1. Press the quilt top, using a damp pressing cloth to protect and steam the wool.

2. Trim the batting and backing even with the edges of the quilt top. Use the 2¼"-wide striped strips to make and attach a double-fold binding.

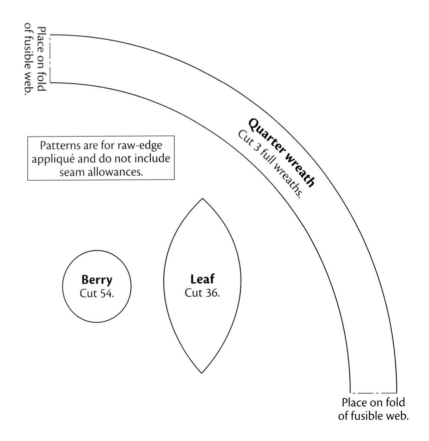

Place on fold of fusible web.

Patterns are for raw-edge appliqué and do not include seam allowances.

Quarter wreath
Cut 3 full wreaths.

Berry
Cut 54.

Leaf
Cut 36.

Place on fold of fusible web.

Kansas in late summer is full of sunflower fields," reports designer Lynne Hagmeier. "We cut them for arranging, hang and dry them for the birds, and roast the seeds for snacking." In this quilt, the sunflowers reflect a wonderful glow in rich golds, browns, greens, and rusts . . . and they couldn't be easier to grow. (All of the fabrics are Lynne's own designs; see "Resources" on page 91.) Flower heads are Courthouse Steps blocks surrounded by triangle squares in a look reminiscent of the classic Kansas Troubles pattern. Leaves are raw-edge appliquéd in woven flannel fabrics so that the soft edges can ravel and, as Lynne says, "hint of their wild natures." Every time you wash the quilt, the edges will get more shaggy.

This design has perfect symmetry for a table runner. Consider cultivating a row of Skinny Quilts, with sunflower heads at the top of stems in different lengths! Or, make one sunflower on an extra-long stem, stitch a tape measure along one side, and use as a growth chart for some especially beloved "early bloomers"!

SUNFLOWER Duet

**By Lynne Hagmeier of Kansas Troubles Quilters;
machine quilted by Nancy Arnoldy**

Finished measurements: 15½" x 54½"

MATERIALS

Yardages are based on fabrics that measure 42" wide. Fat quarters measure 18" x 21". Fat eighths measure 9" x 21".

⅝ yard of tan print for background

½ yard of brown small-scale print for blocks and outer border

¼ yard of rust plaid for blocks and inner border

¼ yard of dark green plaid flannel for stem and leaves

Fat quarter of gold print for blocks

Fat eighth of brown plaid for blocks

Fat eighth of medium green plaid flannel for leaves

Scrap of dark brown mini-scale print for blocks

⅓ yard of brown tone-on-tone print for binding

1¾ yards of fabric for backing

20" x 59" piece of batting

Threads to match fabrics for machine quilting

Freezer paper

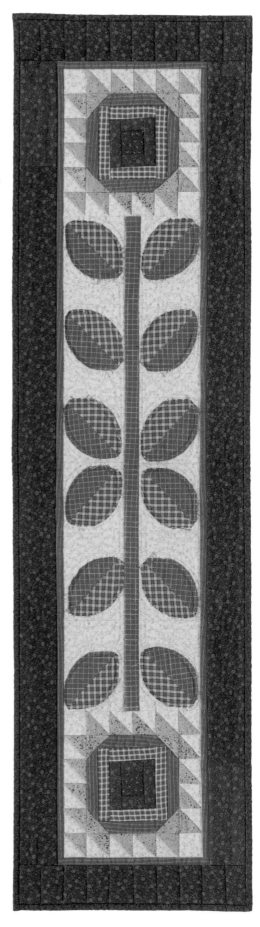

CUTTING

Cut all strips on the crosswise grain of the fabric (selvage to selvage) unless instructed otherwise.

From the scrap of dark brown mini-scale print, cut:
2 squares, 2" x 2"

From the brown small-scale print, cut:
1 strip, 1¼" x 42"; crosscut into:

    4 rectangles, 1¼" x 2"

    4 rectangles, 1¼" x 3½"

4 strips, 3" x 42"

From the brown plaid, cut:
4 rectangles, 1¼" x 3½"

4 rectangles, 1¼" x 5"

From the rust plaid, cut:
2 strips, 1¼" x 42"; crosscut into:

    4 rectangles, 1¼" x 5"

    4 rectangles, 1¼" x 6½"

3 strips, 1" x 42"

From the gold print, cut:
8 squares, 2" x 2"

18 squares, 2⅜" x 2⅜"

From the tan print, cut:
2 strips, 2⅜" x 42"; crosscut into 18 squares, 2⅜" x 2⅜"

2 strips, 2" x 42"; crosscut into:

    4 squares, 2" x 2"

    8 rectangles, 2" x 4½"

2 strips, 4⅞" x 42"; crosscut into 12 squares, 4⅞" x 4⅞". Cut each square in half once diagonally to yield 2 half-square triangles (24 total).

From the dark green plaid flannel, cut:
1 strip, 1½" x 30½"

From the brown tone-on-tone print, cut:
4 strips, 2½" x 42"

From the *lengthwise grain* of the backing fabric, cut:
1 piece, 20" x 59"

MAKING THE SUNFLOWER BLOCKS

The center portion of the Sunflower block is constructed in the same manner as the traditional Courthouse Steps. Finger-press the seams away from the block center as you go.

1. Sew a 1¼" x 2" brown small-scale print rectangle to the top and bottom edges of a 2" brown mini-print square as shown; finger-press. Sew a 1¼" x 3½" brown small-scale print rectangle to the sides of the unit; finger-press. Make two.

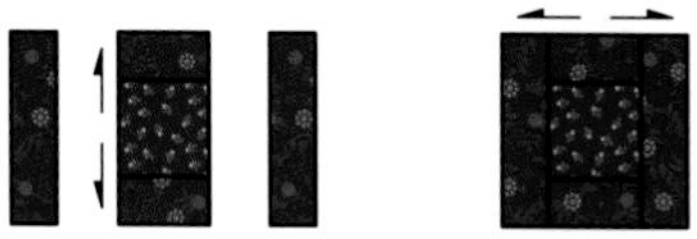

Make 2.

2. Use the method described in step 1 to sew the 1¼" x 3½ and 1¼" x 5" brown plaid rectangles to the units from step 1 as shown; finger-press. Sew the 1¼" x 5" and 1¼" x 6½" rust rectangles to the units; finger-press. Make two.

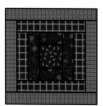

Make 2.

3. Use a pencil to draw a diagonal line on the wrong side of each 2" gold square. With right sides together and raw edges aligned, place a marked square on each corner of a unit from step 2 as shown. Stitch directly on the marked lines. Trim ¼" beyond the stitching line; press. Make two.

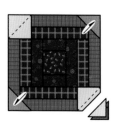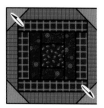

Make 2.

4. Use a pencil to mark a diagonal line on the wrong side of each 2³/₈" tan square. With right sides together and raw edges aligned, place a marked square on a 2³/₈" gold square; pin. Make 18. Stitch a scant ¼" from both sides of the line. Cut on the line to separate the sewn units; press. Make 36 half-square-triangle units.

Make 18.　　　　Make 36.

5. Sew four units from step 4 together as shown; press. Make four of each.

Make 4.　　　　Make 4.

6. Arrange a unit from step 3, two of each unit from step 5, and two 2" tan squares as shown. Sew the units and squares into rows; press. Sew the rows together; press. Make two blocks.

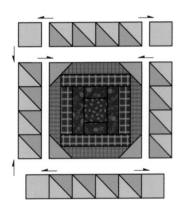

Make 2.

MAKING THE LEAVES

1. Use the half-leaf pattern on page 41 to make a template. Trace 12 leaves onto a piece of freezer paper and cut the leaves out directly on the traced lines.

2. With the waxy side down, press the freezer-paper half-leaves onto the right side of the medium green flannel, with the long straight edge of the paper pattern on the bias of the fabric as shown. Cut out the leaves along the edge of the paper. Peel the freezer

paper from the leaves and repeat to cut 12 leaves from the remaining dark green flannel.

3. Position each half-leaf on a 4⁷/₈" tan half-square triangle, centering and aligning the straight edge of the leaf along the diagonal raw edge of the triangle as shown; pin. Make 12 of each.

Make 12 of each.

4. With right sides together, pin one medium green and one dark green flannel half-leaf unit from step 3 together along the diagonal edges; sew. Unfold and press the seam allowances open. Make 12. You will secure the raw edges later, after the layers of the quilt are basted for quilting.

Make 12.

ASSEMBLING THE QUILT TOP

Work on a large, flat surface such as a design wall, a table, or floor.

1. Arrange the pieced leaf squares, the 2" x 4½" tan rectangles, and the 1½" x 30½" dark green flannel strip as shown in the assembly diagram. Sew the leaf squares and rectangles together into rows; press. Sew a row to opposite long sides of the dark green strip; press.

2. Sew a Sunflower block to each end of the unit from step 1, taking care to position the blocks as shown; press.

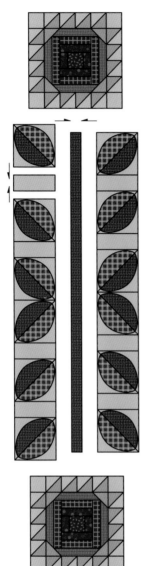

Assembly diagram

3. Sew the 1"-wide rust inner-border strips end to end with diagonal seams to make one long strip. Measure the length of the quilt top through the center. Cut two inner-border strips to this measurement. Pin and sew one strip to each long side of the quilt. Press the seam allowances toward the border.

4. Measure the width of the quilt through the center, including the borders just added. Repeat step 3 to trim, pin, and sew an inner-border strip to the top and bottom edges of the quilt top; press.

5. Sew the 3"-wide brown small-scale print outer-border strips end to end with diagonal seams to make one long strip. Use the method described in steps 3 and 4 to measure, trim, pin, and sew the outer-border strips to the quilt. Press the seam allowances toward the newly added border.

FINISHING

Refer to "Quiltmaking Basics" on page 87 as needed.

1. Press the quilt top. Layer the backing, batting, and quilt top; baste.

2. Quilt as desired or as follows, using thread that matches the fabrics. Machine quilt in the ditch around each round of strips and each triangle of the Sunflower block, and along the stem and the borders. Secure the leaves by straight stitching ¼" from the raw edges with green thread, and then add echo quilting. Quilt the borders with straight lines spaced 1½" apart.

3. Trim the quilt batting and backing even with the edge of the quilt top. Use the 2¼"-wide brown tone-on-tone strips to make and attach a double-fold binding.

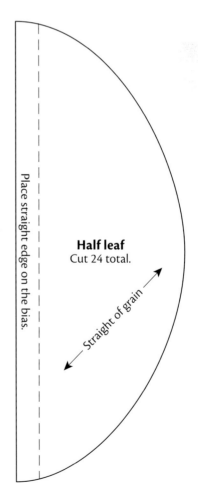

Straight edge of pattern includes seam allowance; curved edge is a cutting line.

Place straight edge on the bias.

Half leaf
Cut 24 total.

Straight of grain

A Garden of SEASONS

Create a sumptuous floral wreath in warm felted wool to beautify your table year-round. Barb Cribb of Wild Thymes Pattern Co. picked the trillium and the rose from her Block of the Month patterns, added yellow stock and sprigs of blue juniper berries, and set them all into a woody vine. Barb is heartfelt in encouraging quilters to work with felted wool: *"It is soothing, like comfort food; it just makes you feel calm and relaxed."* And, since the edges of felted wool don't ravel, she adds, *"The best part is not having to turn under the appliqué pieces!"* Barb hand-dyes her own wool in organic shades (see "Resources" on page 91) and lavishes on lots of embroidery and beading for lush, dimensional effects.

By Barb Cribb of Wild Thymes Pattern Co.

Finished measurements: 18" x 52"

MATERIALS

Fabrics are prefelted, 100% woven wool that measures approximately 54" wide unless otherwise noted. Fat quarters measure 18" x 21". See "Resources," or refer to page 34 for instructions for making your own felted wool.

1¼ yards of moss green wool for outer background and backing

½ yard of black wool for inner background

Fat quarter *each* of 3 different brown wools for vines

Fat quarter of white wool for flowers

7" x 9" piece *each* of 4 shades of spring green wool for leaves*

7" x 9" piece *each* of 4 shades of mint green wool for leaves*

7" x 9" piece *each* of 4 shades of pink wool for flowers*

7" x 9" piece *each* of 4 shades of rose wool for flowers*

7" x 9" piece *each* of 4 shades of red wool for flowers*

7" x 9" piece *each* of 4 shades of yellow wool for flowers*

Wool may be solid, tweed, or subtle plaid.

EMBELLISHMENTS AND TOOLS

Embroidery floss (6-strand) in assorted colors (such as greens, pinks, roses, reds, white, and black)

1 tube *each* of large glass seed beads (also called pebble beads) in blue, pink, yellow and pink, gold, and clear

Embroidery needle that will slip through a pebble bead

Yardstick and either a yardstick compass set or string, pencil, and pushpin**

2 large sheets of paper (18" x 18" minimum)

**Compass sets are available at art, drafting, and office-supply stores.*

Simplify, Simplify!

For a quicker project, create a garland with just a few flowers at each end of your oval runner.

CUTTING

Cut pieces across the width of the fabric unless instructed otherwise.

From the black wool, cut:
1 rectangle, 14" x 46"

From the moss green wool, cut:
2 rectangles, 20" x 52"

From the 18" edge of the 3 brown wools, cut a total of:
³⁄₈"-wide strips to total approximately 400"

From the assorted 7" x 9" yellow wool pieces, cut:
12 strips, ³⁄₄" x 9"; freehand-cut approximately 85 circles, ³⁄₄" in diameter

ASSEMBLING THE BACKGROUND

1. Draft a 12" semicircle and an 18" semicircle onto large sheets of paper. One way to do this is with a yardstick compass. Follow the instructions on the packaging to draw each semicircle on a separate large sheet of paper.

Embroidery Stitches

- As a general rule, choose floss colors that are two shades lighter or darker than the fabrics you are embroidering.

- Unless otherwise indicated, separate the embroidery floss into strands and use three strands at a time in the embroidery needle.

- Knot the end of the thread; hide the knot by coming up through the background fabric.

- Try to keep the strands side by side on the surface of your work; from time to time, let your needle dangle to untwist the strands.

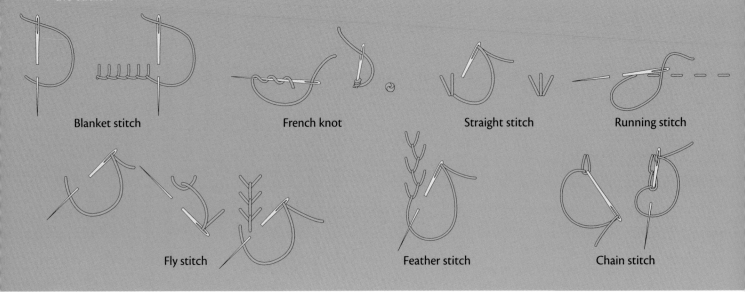

Blanket stitch   French knot   Straight stitch   Running stitch

Fly stitch   Feather stitch   Chain stitch

If you do not have a yardstick compass, tie a length of string around a pencil. Measure 12" along the string, and place a pushpin through the string. Place the pushpin near the bottom edge of the paper and, keeping the string taut, draw a semicircle. Repeat, measuring 18" along the string, to make the larger semicircle.

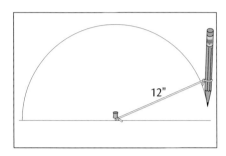

2. Cut out each semicircle template you created in step 1. Pin the 12" semicircle template to one end of the 14" x 46" black rectangle and cut along the curve. Repeat to cut a curve on the opposite end of the rectangle. Use the 18" semicircle template to cut curves on one 20" x 52" green rectangle.

3. Use the green oval you created in step 2 as a template to cut the remaining 20" x 52" green rectangle to the identical size and shape.

4. Center the black oval on one green oval, leaving a 3" margin of green showing all around; pin. Use a blanket stitch and medium green floss to stitch the black oval in place through both layers.

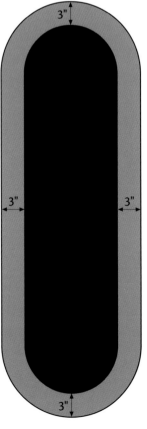

5. Refer to the quilt photo on page 43 to position the assorted 3/8"-wide brown strips, snaking them over the edge between the black and green backgrounds. Take three turns around the background with the strands. There is no need to overlap the ends of the strips; most will be covered by a flower or leaf. Simply pin them in place for now.

Refer to "Embroidery Stitches" on page 44 and "My Beading Heart" on page 46 as needed. To stay organized, separate the flower shapes and store them in labeled zip-lock bags, one for each type of flower.

1. Use the patterns on page 47 to make templates for the leaf (A), trillium (B–F), and rose (G–I).

2. Use the leaf template to cut 47 A pieces from the assorted spring green and mint green wool pieces. Cut some leaves a little larger all around for variety.

3. Use the trillium templates to cut a total of five B pieces from the lightest pink wool pieces; five C pieces from the more medium pink pieces; five D pieces from the darkest pink wool pieces; five E pieces from the white wool; and five F pieces from the assorted mint green wool pieces.

4. Layer and center a B piece over a C piece and secure by stitching three pink beads in the center. Center the B-C unit over a D piece and use embroidery floss and a blanket stitch to finish the edges of C while securing it to D. Center the B-C-D unit over an E piece and use a blanket stitch to finish the edges of D while securing it to E. Finish the edges of E with a blanket stitch and white floss. Make five and set the trillium units plus the loose F pieces aside.

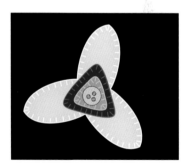

Make 5.

5. Use the rose templates to cut a total of 9 G pieces from the lightest pink, rose, and red wool pieces; 9 H pieces from the more medium pink, rose, and red pieces; and 18 I pieces from the darkest pink, rose, and red pieces.

6. Layer a G piece over an H piece as indicated by the dashed line on the pattern. Finish the top, curved edge of G with embroidery floss and a blanket stitch while securing it to H. Use long straight stitches to create

stamens, finishing each with a coordinating bead as shown. Make nine embellished roses and set them aside along with the loose I petals.

Make 9.

ARRANGING THE FLOWERS AND LEAVES

Refer to the quilt photo on page 43 for guidance as needed. Work on a large, flat surface such as a design wall, a table, or floor.

1. Layer each trillium unit over an F piece. Arrange the units asymmetrically on the background. Avoid placing a trillium directly on top of a vine; pin. Next, position the rose units, placing some over the end of a vine.

2. Cluster and overlap 12 to 16 assorted yellow circles, ranging from dark to light, in a pyramid shape over the ends of or alongside the vines; pin. Make six clusters.

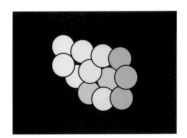

Make 6.

3. Add the assorted green A leaves—singly, or in pairs or trios—radiating outward from flowers and vines; pin.

4. Rearrange the elements as desired to produce a balanced composition.

STITCHING THE ELEMENTS

1. Refer to "Embroidery Stitches" on page 44. Use floss in a variety of brown and green shades to stitch the vines to the background with stitches such as the running stitch, blanket stitch, chain stitch, and fly stitch.

2. Stitch the leaves in place, using green floss and a blanket stitch for the edges and straight stitches for the veins. Occasionally, blanket stitch the edge of a leaf without securing it to the background for added texture and dimension.

3. Use green floss and a blanket stitch to secure each F piece to the background, blanket-stitching one lobe of the leaf while leaving it loose from the background. Use white floss to tack the flower unit securely on top, offsetting the petals.

Embroidery and beading add texture and sparkle.

4. Blanket-stitch each rose unit to the background across the rose's top scalloped edge using floss in a matching or coordinating color. Place an I petal piece on either side of each rose as indicated by the dashed lines on the pattern; finish with a blanket stitch through several layers to secure.

My Beading Heart

- Add beads as you embroider, using the same three strands of embroidery floss. If you are starting with a bead, bring the needle up from the back and take a backstitch before adding the bead.

- Pass the threaded needle through one bead at a time, and then insert the needle into the background. Each bead should stand on its side, like a car tire, so the holes in the beads are not obvious.

- Reinsert the needle into the background, then add another bead, or finish off with a backstitch directly under the bead. Insert the needle and bring it up at least an inch away, then clip the thread ends close to the surface.

5. Stitch two or three yellow, pink-and-yellow, or gold beads to each yellow stock circle, sewing through to the background to secure each circle in place.

Try This!

If you prefer, substitute French knots for the beads in the center of each yellow stock circle.

6. Use green floss and blue beads to fill in background areas as desired with delicate, feather-stitched juniper sprigs.

FINISHING

1. Place the embellished piece on the remaining green oval. This provides a backing to hide the knots, stitches, and thread ends and to give the finished piece extra depth and stability. Use green embroidery floss to work a blanket stitch all around the exterior edge to attach the backing.

2. Use three strands of black floss to quilt a few large S curves randomly over the black oval center of the table runner.

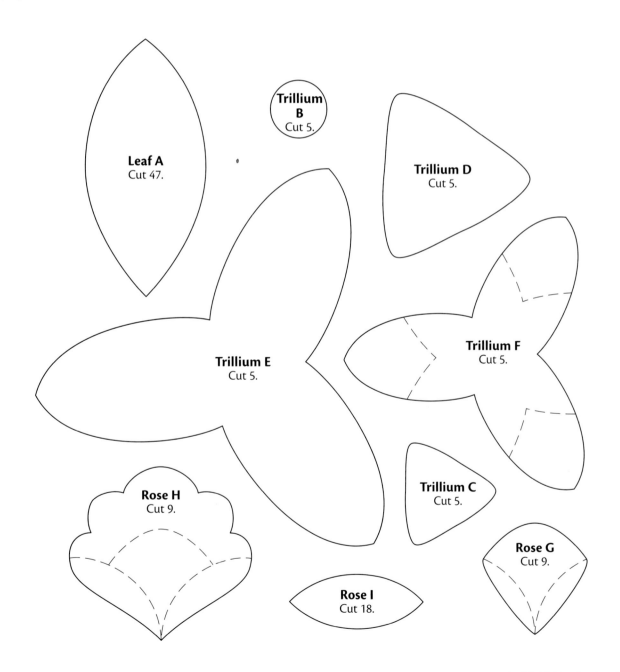

SHERBET with Every Meal

Linda Pool loves lace—along with metal filigree, gingerbread wooden molding, and sometimes even die-cut plastic! *"There is a simple beauty in openwork and so much inspiration for quilt design,"* she rhapsodizes. Her favorite technique for expressing her passion is cutwork appliqué, a form of reverse appliqué. Linda cuts shapes into a top layer, then needle turns the edges to reveal one or more fabrics underneath. *"The more you cut and stitch,"* she explains, *"the more of the design you get to see."*

True to her fashion and taste, Linda sticks with hand appliqué and hand quilting. That's not to say that machine appliqué and machine quilting wouldn't be effective, nor that this table runner wouldn't look heavenly in black, with jewel-tones peeking through the cutwork. However, Linda has chosen to serve up various hand-dyed fabrics in raspberry, strawberry, pistachio, and lemon under a fresh white tone-on-tone top layer. Think small dishes of sherbet for cleansing the palate between courses of an elegant luncheon or dinner!

By Linda Pool

Finished measurements: 14½" x 62½"

MATERIALS

Yardages are based on fabrics that measure 42" wide. Fat quarters measure 18" x 21".

2 yards of white tone-on-tone print for quilt top

Fat quarter *each* of rose, pink, light green, and yellow hand-dyed fabrics or subtle prints for reverse appliqués

2 yards of light green print for backing

White thread for reverse appliqué

Thread to match one of the fat quarters for hand quilting

18" x 64" piece of thin, bonded batting

Black and blue medium-point permanent markers

Tracing paper

Freezer paper

Spray starch or sizing

No. 2 pencil, well sharpened

Small, sharp scissors

Chopstick or large crochet hook

Hand-appliqué needle

Craft knife, such as XACTO, with #11 blade (optional)

CUTTING

For this quilt, cut all strips on the lengthwise grain *of the fabric (parallel to the selvage) unless instructed otherwise.*

From the white tone-on-tone print, cut:

1 rectangle, 18" x 64"

From the light green print, cut:

1 rectangle, 6" x 16"

1 rectangle, 18" x 64"

CREATING THE PATTERN

1. Make color photocopies or use markers to trace each full-sized pattern on pages 52–55 onto a separate sheet of tracing paper. Make two center vine patterns, rotate one 180°, align along dashed lines, and tape together.

2. Use a pencil and a large square or rectangular quilter's ruler to draw a 14½" x 62½" rectangle on the dull side of a piece of freezer paper, making sure that the corners are perfect 90° angles. Cut out the rectangle directly on the drawn lines.

3. Fold the freezer-paper rectangle lengthwise and crosswise in half, crease the folds to mark the centers, and then unfold it. Place the border repeat pattern under the freezer paper so that dashed line A is aligned with the crosswise crease and the dotted line is aligned with the top cut edge of the rectangle. Use a light box or other light source to see the markings. Use a black marker to trace the black lines, and pencil or blue marker for the dashed lines.

4. Move the freezer paper 6" to the left, realign the dotted line of the pattern with the top edge of the freezer paper, and align dashed line A with the dashed line B of the border repeat. Trace as before. Repeat to draw a total of four segments or until you get to within 7¼" of the right edge of the freezer paper.

5. Trace the corner border pattern on the right edge of the freezer paper, aligning the dashed B lines and the dotted line as before, and also aligning dashed line C on the lengthwise crease. Trace the corner border pattern to complete one quarter of the border design.

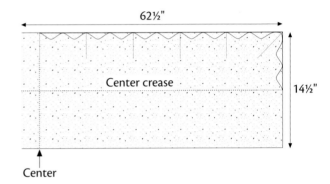

6. Refold the freezer paper as before, with the marked quarter on top. Pin or staple a few areas to keep the layers from shifting. Cut out along the marked scalloped edge, through all four layers; unfold.

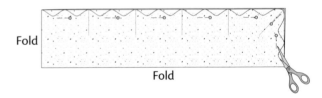

7. Transfer the appliqué shapes to the other quarters of the freezer paper. First, fold the freezer paper in half crosswise, align the scalloped edges, and trace the appliqués. To complete the border design, fold the freezer paper in half lengthwise, again aligning the scallops, and trace the appliqués.

8. Transfer the center vine pattern to the freezer paper, aligning the blue dashed lines with the center creases. Trace the sherbet drops pattern at both ends of the marked vine, aligning the blue dashed lines and the lengthwise crease. Refer to the quilt photo on page 49 for guidance as needed.

TRANSFERRING THE PATTERN TO FABRIC

1. Using spray starch or sizing spray, press and straighten the 18" x 64" white print rectangle.

2. Center the freezer-paper pattern, waxy side down, on the wrong side of the pressed rectangle. Press lightly with a dry, hot iron to adhere the pattern in place.

3. Working over a light box or other light source, use a sharp No. 2 pencil to trace all black design lines lightly onto the right side of the white rectangle. Carefully peel off the freezer-paper pattern; set it aside for the quilting phase.

CUTWORK AND NEEDLE-TURN APPLIQUÉ

1. Using a craft knife and working on a cutting mat—or, if you prefer, using small, sharp scissors—cut a small slit in the white rectangle in the center of every marked appliqué shape. *Do not* cut out any shapes yet.

2. Position the 6" x 16" green rectangle behind the center vine area of the white rectangle. Pin and then baste about 3/16" outside the marked line of the shape with a loose running stitch.

3. Slip the point of small, sharp scissors into the slit you cut into the vine shape in step 1. Extend the slit 1" outward to both sides, along the lengthwise center stem of the vine, maintaining a 1/8" seam allowance between the cut edge and the pencil line. Cut away the white fabric within the shape, leaving a 1/8" to 3/16" seam allowance along the pencil lines. Clip almost up to the pencil line along curves—at intervals as small as 1/8" along the sharpest curves—and also at the inside points.

4. Thread an appliqué needle with white thread; knot the end. Bring the needle up from the back of the piece and into the turned-under edge of the top fabric. Use the tip of the needle to sweep the seam allowance under. When you can no longer see the marked pencil line, secure the turned-under seam allowance with your left thumbnail if you are right-handed or with your right thumbnail if you are left-handed. Use tiny stitches along one edge of the vine's center stem, appliquéing the white folded edge to the green fabric beneath it.

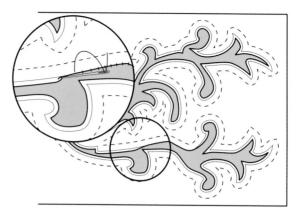

Reverse appliqué with needle-turn method

5. When you've finished stitching both halves of the center vine, turn the piece over and trim away the green fabric 1/4" beyond the appliqué stitches. Referring to the quilt photo on page 49 and the patterns, work reverse appliqué for all other green areas throughout the quilt top. Repeat to add the pink, yellow, and then the rose reverse-appliqué shapes.

CREATING THE SCALLOPED EDGE

1. For stability, stay stitch by machine just outside the traced scalloped line all around the edge of the quilt top. Press and block the top so it is as straight and square as possible.

2. Layer the appliquéd quilt, right side up; the 18" x 64" green backing rectangle, right side down; and the batting. Pin.

3. Turn the sandwich over so the wrong side of the quilt top is facing you. Machine stitch the entire way around the quilt just inside the line of stay stitches you made in step 1. Trim 1/4" beyond the new stitching, and clip the curves, taking care not to cut into the stitching.

Original stitching
New stitching
Quilt back

4. Make a 3" slash in the back of the quilt batting and backing fabric, about 2" to 3" from the edge of the scalloped seam on one short edge of the quilt. Carefully turn the quilt right side out. Smooth out each scallop from the inside, using the tip of a chopstick or large crochet hook. Press, making sure the green backing does not show on the front of the quilt.

5. Bring the edges of the slashed batting together without overlapping them, and stitch the slash closed with a few long cross-stitches. Repeat to close the opening in the backing fabric. Don't worry: you can cover the stitches with a quilt label when you are finished quilting (see "At the Finish Line" on page 91).

QUILTING

Refer to "Quiltmaking Basics" on page 87 as needed. Quilt as desired or as follows: use a contrasting thread to stitch ¼" from the scalloped edge to flatten it and to serve as decorative topstitching. Quilt each reverse appliqué shape *just* inside the fold line of the white fabric to delicately outline each motif. Cut out the vine from the freezer-paper pattern, center it waxy side down between the sherbet drop and each short end of the quilt, press it in place, and quilt along the outside edges of the pattern. (Adapt as necessary to fit.) Fill any remaining areas with echo quilting.

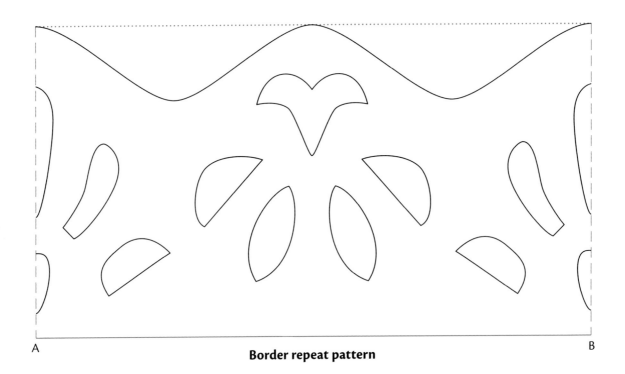

A
Border repeat pattern
B

Corner border pattern

B

C

Place along lengthwise crease of freezer paper.

Sherbet drop

Rotate pattern 180° along this line.

Center vine

C are for a spot of tea? Like almost all of Laura Wasilowski's work, this runner is made from her own hand-dyed fabrics (see "Resources" on page 91), is machine quilted, and celebrates the humble images of her domestic life with wit, whimsy, and bright color. Motifs are fused, because for Laura, *"Fusing is the most direct route from an idea in my head to the implementation of that idea."*

Pour out your hearty sense of fun as you make this runner in the morning and complete it in time to set the table for 4 o'clock high tea.

By Laura Wasilowski

Finished measurements: 15" x 44"

MATERIALS

Yardages are based on fabrics that measure 42" wide.
Fat quarters measure 18" x 21".

1⅝ yards of lime green hand-dyed or solid fabric for background

½ yard of peach hand-dyed or similar fabric with variegations of bright rose and purple for teapot, teacup, saucer, and flower-center appliqués, and binding

Fat quarter of mottled turquoise hand-dyed fabric for square appliqués

Scraps of turquoise solid for flower designs

1⅝ yards of fabric for backing

17" x 46" piece of batting

4½ yards of 18"-wide lightweight paper-backed fusible web

Peach, dark green, and turquoise threads for machine quilting

Decorative rotary-cutter blades, such as pinking, scallop, or wave (optional)

Lead pencil or fine-tip permanent marker

PREPARING THE FABRICS

1. Cut a 17" x 46" piece from the *lengthwise grain* of both the lime green and backing fabrics.

2. Following the manufacturer's instructions, apply the fusible web to the wrong side (if applicable) of the pieces you cut in step 1, as well as the variegated peach, mottled turquoise, and solid turquoise fabrics. When the adhesive has cooled, remove the paper backing from each fabric in one piece if possible. Retain this paper, called release paper, for tracing and fusing.

3. Place the variegated fabric, fusible side up, on your cutting board. With a decorative blade in the rotary cutter if desired, cut four strips, 1¼" x 42". Set these strips aside for binding.

Protect Your Cutting Mat

Decorative rotary blades are fun, but they can nick your cutting mat. Use the ungridded, reverse side of the mat, or keep an old mat in your sewing room just for use with decorative blades.

4. Place the 17" x 46" piece of backing fabric, fusible side up, on a large pressing surface. Center the batting, then the 17" x 46" piece of lime green fabric, fusible side down, on top. Fuse-tack the layers in place as described in the tip below.

No Pins! No Thread!

Fuse-tacking temporarily secures fabric prepped with fusible web to another fabric without the need to pin or baste. Simply apply a hot iron for *just* three to five seconds to the prepared fabric. Fuse the fabric permanently when you are satisfied with the placement and ready to move ahead.

CUTTING THE MOTIFS

1. Place the release paper you retained while preparing the fabrics over the teapot pattern on page 60. Trace all outlines except those for the flower and flower center with a lead pencil or fine-tip permanent marker.

2. Roughly cut out the main body of the teapot and lid pattern. Choose a section of variegated fabric that features curved, soft shading suggesting a rounded surface. Place the paper tracing from step 1, marked side down, on the fabric, fusible side up. Using a pressing cloth or unmarked piece of release paper, fuse-tack the paper to the fabric for five seconds. Let the fabric cool.

3. Carefully remove the paper tracing from the fabric. The lead or ink will be transferred to the melted fusible web on the fabric.

4. Use sharp scissors to cut out the teapot and lid shapes just *inside* the traced line.

5. Use the method described in steps 2–4 to trace and cut out the teapot spout, handle, and knob from slightly contrasting areas of the variegated fabric.

6. Repeat steps 2–5 to cut and trace a second teapot, using the same marked release-paper pieces.

7. Use the method described in steps 1–5 to trace and cut out two teacups and two saucers. Cut the cups, cup rims, cup handles, and outer saucer shapes from areas of one color, and the inside saucer shapes from areas of contrasting colors.

8. Place the paper tracings for the main teapot and teacup shapes onto the corresponding patterns on page 60 and trace the flower and flower center. Use these patterns to trace and cut two large flowers and two small flowers from the prepared turquoise solid. (If you prefer, you can cut these pieces freehand.) Cut two flower centers from a peach area of the variegated fabric for the flower centers.

9. Place the mottled turquoise fabric, fusible side up, on your cutting mat. Use a decorative scalloped rotary blade if desired and, working freehand or with an acrylic ruler, cut four strips, 1½" x 18". Line the strips up alongside each other—stacking will cause them to stick together—and crosscut them into a total of 46 squares, 1½" x 1½".

FUSING AND QUILTING

Refer to "Quiltmaking Basics" on page 87 as needed.

1. Refer to the quilt photo on page 57 or use your imagination to arrange the teapots, teacups, saucers, and squares on the background fabric; fuse-tack the pieces in place. Note that the quilt will be trimmed and bound after quilting, so keep the appliqués away from the edges. When you are ready, press the quilt with steam to set the glue.

2. Quilt as desired or free-motion machine quilt each teapot with peach thread to outline the flower and use an allover pattern to define the roundness of the shapes. Stitch long loops along the spout, handle, and lid, and a spiral on the knob. Quilt each teacup with wavy lines to suggest tea in the background space within the rim. Stitch along the cup rim and handle, within the cup to define the round shape, and around the flower. Work deep looping lines that radiate outward along the inner saucer, and then along the saucer's rim. Finally, quilt an allover design over the checkerboard squares and the background with dark green thread.

It's All about ME

Laura's allover background pattern is a series of squared-off loops that alternate between the vertical (which look like boxy Ms) and horizontal (which look like boxy Es), which is why she calls this the ME-ME-ME pattern!

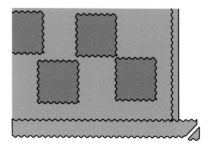

FINISHING

1. Press and block your quilt so it is as straight and square as possible. Square and, if necessary, trim the three layers to measure 15" x 44".

2. Place the quilt right side up and insert a piece of release paper or a pressing sheet underneath. Place one 1¼"-wide variegated strip, fusible side down, on one long edge of the quilt, overlapping the front of the quilt by ½". Fuse-tack in place, shifting the paper or pressing sheet as you go. (You will need a few inches of a second strip to run the entire length of the quilt.) Repeat to fuse a binding strip to the opposite long edge.

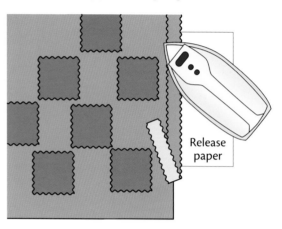

Release paper

3. Fold the binding to the back of the quilt; fuse-tack in place.

4. From the remaining 1¼"-wide strips, cut two strips, 17" long. Center a strip over one short edge of the quilt, overlapping the front of the quilt by ½". (About 1" of binding will extend beyond each corner.) Fuse-tack in place using a protective sheet of release paper or a pressing sheet. Trim a ½" triangle from the binding at each corner, fold the corner under to miter it, and then fold the binding to the back of the quilt. Fuse-tack in place and steam-set the binding.

5. Machine quilt with contrasting thread and a decorative stitch along the raw edges of the binding on the front of the quilt.

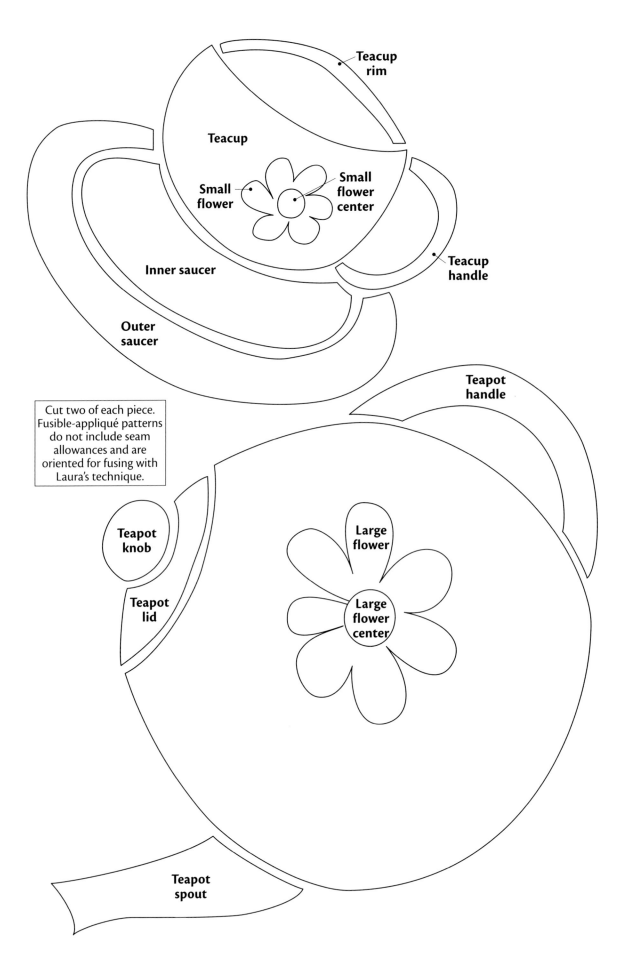

Teacup rim

Teacup

Small flower center

Small flower

Inner saucer

Outer saucer

Teacup handle

Cut two of each piece. Fusible-appliqué patterns do not include seam allowances and are oriented for fusing with Laura's technique.

Teapot handle

Teapot knob

Teapot lid

Large flower

Large flower center

Teapot spout

Karen reflects, *"There's something magical about being at the water's edge. Looking out toward an expansive sky and beautiful cool blue waves and having warm sand at my feet fills me with peace."* This skinny seascape is a version of Karen's "Accidental Landscapes" technique. All it takes to capture the essence of the shore is to cut free-form curves in fabric and layer the strips with topstitching.

Hang the finished masterpiece like a window at a beach house, or display it on a table along with the seashells you've collected.

By the SEA   By Karen Eckmeier

Finished measurements: 12" x 48"

MATERIALS

Unless otherwise indicated, fabrics are 100% cotton in tone-on-tones and other quiet prints, as well as variegated hand-dyes. Fat quarters measure 18" x 21".

½ yard of mottled tan print for sand

⅓ yard of light blue-and-white print or hand-dyed fabric for sky*

⅓ yard of white solid or white-on-white print for surf

⅛ yard *each* of 4 dark blue, 4 dark teal, 4 medium blue, 4 medium turquoise, 2 light blue, and 3 light aqua solids, subtle prints, or hand-dyed fabrics for water

⅛ yard *each* of light blue and green lamé fabrics for water

1½ yards of turquoise batik for backing and binding

14" x 50" piece of cotton batting

⅜ yard of gold tulle

½ yard of 2"-wide flat white lace trim

Threads to match fabrics for topstitching and machine quilting

1 yard *each* of 3 or 4 different blue and green novelty yarns and trims

Fabric glue with applicator tip

A few pearl, gold seed, and gold pebble beads

Beading needle

Assortment of small seashells

Chalk pencil (optional)

If this fabric has a directional pattern that runs vertically, purchase ½ yard.

CUTTING

Cut all strips on the crosswise grain of the fabric (selvage to selvage) unless instructed otherwise.

From the light blue-and-white sky print or hand-dyed fabric, cut:*
1 rectangle, 9" x 14"

From the mottled tan fabric, cut:
1 rectangle, 17" x 14"

From the white solid or white-on-white print, cut:
3 strips, 4" x 18"

From *each* dark blue and dark teal solid, subtle print, or hand-dyed fabric, cut:
1 strip, 2" x 14" (8 total)

From *each* medium blue and medium turquoise solid, subtle print, or hand-dyed fabric, cut:
1 strip, 3" x 15" (8 total)

From *each* light blue and light aqua solid, subtle print, or hand-dyed fabric, cut:
1 strip, 4" x 18" (5 total)

From *each* lamé fabric, cut:
1 strip, 4" x 18" (2 total)

From the *lengthwise grain* of the turquoise batik, cut:
1 rectangle, 16" x 52"

3 strips, 2¼" x 52"

*If this fabric has a directional pattern that runs vertically, cut it on the lengthwise grain.

PREPARING THE PIECES

1. Set the darkest blue 2" x 14" strip aside. Use a rotary cutter to cut a free-form gentle curve along one long edge of each remaining 2" x 14" dark blue and dark teal strip; each 3" x 15" medium blue and medium turquoise strip; and each 4" x 18" light blue and light aqua, lamé, and white strip. Make a different curve each time: a very shallow curve on the 2"-wide strips, a less shallow curve on the 3" strips, and more swooping curves on the 4"-wide strips as shown. Avoid wavy lines, as they are hard to press. Practice on scrap fabric; if you still feel uncomfortable cutting freehand, draw the curves with a chalk pencil before you cut.

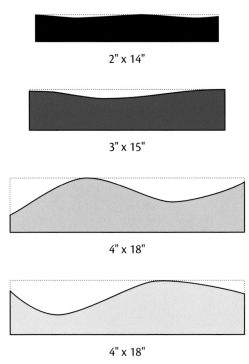

2" x 14"

3" x 15"

4" x 18"

4" x 18"

2. Place each curved strip from step 1 right side down on an ironing surface and gently press ¼" along the curved edge to the back of the fabric. To do this, lightly pinch the curved fabric edge with your index finger underneath and your thumb on top, and let the fabric edge glide through your fingers as you follow with the tip of the iron as shown. Also press ¼" to the back along one long edge of the dark blue strip you set aside.

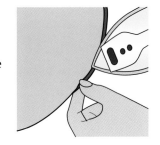

3. Referring to the quilt photo on page 61 for guidance as needed, arrange the strips from step 2 by value and width, with the darkest, narrowest strips at the top and the lightest, widest strips at the bottom.

LAYERING THE SEASCAPE

Work on a large, flat surface such as a design wall, a table, or floor. Refer to the quilt photo for guidance as needed.

1. Place the 14" x 50" piece of batting on a flat surface, with the short edges at the top and bottom, for use as a foundation.

2. With right sides up and aligning the top and side edges, place the 9" x 14" blue-and-white rectangle for the sky on the batting; pin. For the sand in the foreground, place the 17" x 14" tan rectangle right side up on the batting, aligning the bottom and side edges; pin.

3. Beginning from the bottom, place the curved edge of one 4" x 18" white strip on the diagonal, right side up, over the top edge of the tan piece as shown; pin. The left edge of the white strip should be approximately 8" from the bottom edge of the tan fabric.

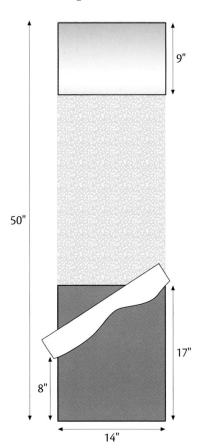

4. Overlap the lightest blue or aqua strip on top of the white strip with the pressed curve along the bottom and at the same 45° angle, allowing about 1½" to 2" of the white fabric to show. Repeat to layer the remaining light and white strips, leaving 1½" to 2" between the curvy edges. Try different sequences of strips until you are pleased with the flow of colors and the balance of curves. It's OK for the curve of one strip to overlap the previous strip and touch the one before one that.

5. Layer the medium strips in the same way, gradually changing the angle from 45° to 90° so that the strips at the top of this section are parallel to the top and bottom edges of the batting. At the same time, gradually decrease the distance between strips, so they are approximately 1" to 1½" apart.

6. Set aside a dark teal strip. Take the dark blue strip you *did not* cut into a curve and press one long straight edge ¼" to the wrong side. Place the strip on the batting with the pressed-under edge overlapping the bottom raw edge of the sky fabric by ½". This pressed edge forms the horizon of your seascape.

7. Layer the next darkest strip below and overlapping the first dark strip, this time with the pressed curved edge *on top* (toward the sky), about ½" from the horizon. Continue layering the remaining dark strips, working from the darkest to the least dark, always placing the pressed curve toward the sky, and varying the distance between strips from ½" to 1".

8. Shift pieces as needed so that the raw edges of the top and middle sections meet. Rotary cut a curved edge along the unpressed long edge of the dark teal strip you set aside in step 6, and press under ¼" along the curve. Place this piece on top of the raw edges where the top and middle sections meet as shown.

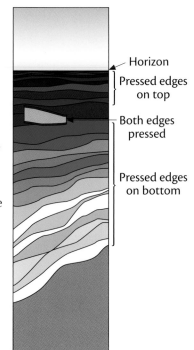

Horizon

Pressed edges on top

Both edges pressed

Pressed edges on bottom

9. Cut a 9"-long piece of white lace trim. Insert the unfinished edge under the white strip that meets the tan fabric along a concave curve, to suggest the foam of the wave as it rolls onto the sand.

TOPSTITCHING

1. Make any desired changes in the order and exposed area of the strips. Pin through to the batting along all pressed curves, inserting pins about 2" apart and perpendicular to the edges.

2. Use white thread and a slightly longer-than-usual straight stitch (about six stitches to the inch) to topstitch along the bottom white strip, 1/8" from the crease of the pressed, curved edge where it overlaps the lace.

3. Using thread to match each fabric, topstitch along the pressed edges of all remaining strips.

ADDING DETAILS AND QUILTING

Refer to "Quiltmaking Basics" on page 87 as needed for these and all remaining steps.

1. Press the quilt top on its batting foundation. Layer this pressed unit over the backing; baste.

2. Use a very thin line of fabric glue to secure a few strands of novelty yarn and trim in curvy lines across the medium and dark strips. Allow the glue to dry; you will secure these embellishments with couching later.

3. Utilize the pattern of the remaining lace trim to cut three curvy V shapes for seagulls. Referring to the quilt photo on page 61 for placement, glue-baste the seagulls to the sky fabric. Alternatively, paint or embroider seagulls.

Gull shapes cut from lace trim.

4. Quilt as desired or as follows: use matching and variegated thread to machine quilt two or three curvy lines on each strip without crossing the lines of topstitching. Use white thread to machine quilt along the lines in the sky fabric and to free-motion stitch a meandering motif and curlicues along the bottom of each white strip for a frothy look. Machine tack the bodies of the lace seagulls, leaving the wings free to fly.

5. Couch the blue and green yarns by straight stitching along the core of each strand with matching thread.

FINISHING

1. Trim and square up the piece to measure 12" x 48", making sure that the horizon is parallel to the top edge of the quilt.

2. Use the 2¼"-wide turquoise strips to make and attach a double-fold binding.

3. Refer to "My Beading Heart" on page 46 as needed and use a beading needle to hand stitch pearl and gold beads to the sand along the white fabric strip.

4. Scatter the seashells over the sand area. Place a 13" square of tulle loosely over the shells. Baste with pins or thread to temporarily hold the shells in place. Machine quilt with tan thread in gently curving lines from one side to the other, encasing each shell. Trim away the excess tulle by carefully cutting 1/8" beyond the quilting lines.

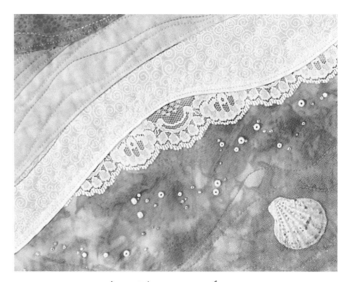

Lace trim suggests foam.

Arnold MARATHON

W hat a gorgeous art quilt this is, with its mix of shimmering silk crazy patches and fantasy flowers. Says the artist, Yvonne Porcella, of her palette of brilliant colors accented with kicky black-and-white checks, *"I see green and brown trees out my windows and like to create my own colorful interior environment."*

But you're probably wondering, "What's with the crazy name?" Yvonne explains that her studio, which looks out onto cedar and pine forest, is located in a California Sierra Mountain area named Arnold. Also, a marathon is marked by a long distance, and someone who runs a marathon is known as a long-distance runner. Enjoying a chance to play with words as well as fabric, she chuckles, *"So a Skinny Quilt could be considered a long runner!"*

Don't mistake this stunner of a runner for a marathon project, though—you can choose to cut most of it freehand and it's quickly fused together.

By Yvonne Porcella

Finished measurements: 15" x 61"

MATERIALS

Yardages are based on fabrics that measure 42" wide unless otherwise noted. Fat quarters measure 18" x 22". Fat eighths measure 9" x 21". See "Resources" on page 91 for silk fabric sources.

Fat quarter or fat eighth *each* of 8 to 10 cottons, dupioni silks, and silk taffetas in assorted red, orange, and purple solids, tone-on-tone prints, and quiet stripes for background and binding

Scraps of 20 to 25 cottons, dupioni silks, and silk taffeta solids, tone-on-tone prints, and subtle prints in assorted greens and other colors to contrast with the background fabrics for flower, leaf, and stem appliqués

Scraps of 2 or 3 black-and-white checkerboard prints in various scales for stem and checkerboard appliqués

2 yards of lightweight cotton, such as batiste, for foundation

2 yards of cotton fabric for backing

²/₃ yard of black-and-white, large-scale checked taffeta or gingham for binding

5¼ yards of 18"-wide fusible web

19" x 64" piece of wool batting

Thread in a darker shade of the main background color for machine appliqué and quilting

Basting spray (optional)

CUTTING

For this quilt, cut all strips on the lengthwise grain *of the fabric (parallel to the selvage) unless instructed otherwise.*

From one of the 8 to 10 cottons, dupioni silks, or silk taffetas in assorted red, orange, and purple solids, tone-on-tone prints, and quiet stripes, cut:
2 strips, 2½" x 15½"

From the *width* **of the fusible web, cut:**
30 strips, 6" x 17"

From the lightweight cotton, such as batiste, cut:
1 piece, 19" x 64"

From the black-and-white, large-scale checked taffeta or gingham, cut:
2½"-wide bias strips to total approximately 132"

From the backing fabric, cut:
1 piece, 19" x 64"

PREPARING THE FABRICS

Refer to "Fusible Appliqué the Easy Way" on page 88 as needed.

1. Cut each red, orange, and purple background fabric along the lengthwise grain into 6½"-wide strips. Fat quarters will yield three strips, 6½" x 18". Fat eighths will yield three strips, 6½" x 9". Set the remaining fabric aside.

2. Follow the manufacturer's instructions to apply fusible web to the wrong side of the background strips you cut in step 1, the scraps of assorted green and other contrasting appliqué fabrics, and the scraps of black-and-white checkerboard prints. Use the 6" x 17" strips of fusible web for the background pieces and the leftovers for the scraps. Then, with the fusible side up, trim any edges that are not backed with fusible web.

MAKING THE CRAZY-PATCH BACKGROUND

Refer to the quilt photo on page 67 for guidance as needed.

1. With the fusible side down and working freehand, rotary cut irregular polygons (multisided pieces) in assorted shapes and sizes from the prepared red, orange, and purple background fabrics. Take a visual estimate and cut enough pieces to cover the 19" x 64" foundation piece of lightweight cotton.

2. Smooth out the 19" x 64" foundation piece on a large, flat ironing surface.

3. With fusible sides down, arrange the cut shapes from step 1, overlapping them so they cover the entire surface of the foundation. Aim for a pleasing balance of colors, fabrics, and shapes. When you are happy with the arrangement, fuse the shapes in place. Use a pressing cloth or nonstick pressing sheet to protect the iron and ironing surface as necessary.

Filling In

Use the paper backing peeled off the fusible web to trace any gaps between the background pieces. Now you'll have patterns, so you can cut oversized fabric patches from the leftover background fabrics and cover these gaps.

4. Square and trim the crazy-patch background to measure 15" x 61".

ADDING THE APPLIQUÉS

Work on a large, flat surface such as a design wall, a table, or floor.

1. Enlarge the patterns on pages 70–71 and use them to make templates for the flowers, leaves, and stems for each flower or group of flowers; or work more intuitively and simply refer to the patterns but cut the pieces freehand.

2. Referring to the quilt photo, cut stems for flowers A and H and various leaves for all the flowers from the prepared green scraps. Cut the petals, flower centers, and so on for all the flowers from the assorted contrasting scraps, and the main stems for flowers A–G from the black-and-white checkerboard fabrics. Refer to the photo or use your imagination to arrange the stems, flowers, and leaves on the crazy-patch background; pin.

3. From each black-and-white checkerboard fabric, cut a few miniature Nine Patch blocks. Place them on the crazy-patch background, turning them at different angles and scattering them between the flowers; pin.

Cut from black-and-white checkerboard fabrics in varying scales to create flower stems and instant Nine Patch appliqué blocks.

4. When you are satisfied with the overall arrangement, fuse the appliqués in place. You will secure the motifs during the quilting process.

FINISHING

Refer to "Quiltmaking Basics" on page 87 as needed.

1. Press and block your quilt top so it is as straight and square as possible. Layer the backing, batting, and quilt top; baste, using basting spray if desired.

2. Quilt as desired or free-motion machine quilt inside and outside the flower shapes and in any open spaces in the background, using thread a shade darker than the main background color.

3. Trim the batting and backing edges even with the edge of the quilt top. Use the 2½"-wide black-and-white bias strips to make a double-fold binding, piecing the strips on an angle that continues the striped pattern. From this long strip, cut two 61"-long strips of binding and sew them to the long edges of the quilt.

4. Center a 15½"-long strip cut from background fabric on the top edge of the quilt. (About ¼" of binding will extend beyond each corner.) Prepare and insert a sleeve for hanging. Sew the binding to the quilt, folding the overhanging raw ends under neatly to the inside of the binding. Repeat to add a 15½"-long binding strip and a sleeve at the bottom of the quilt.

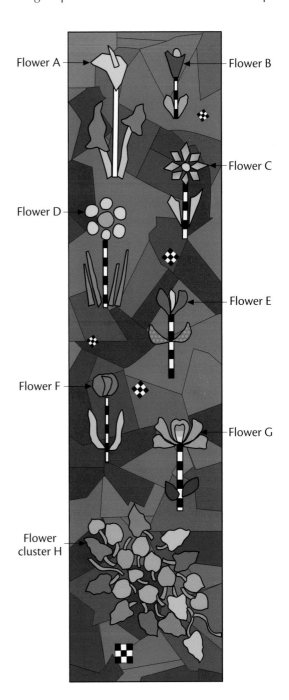

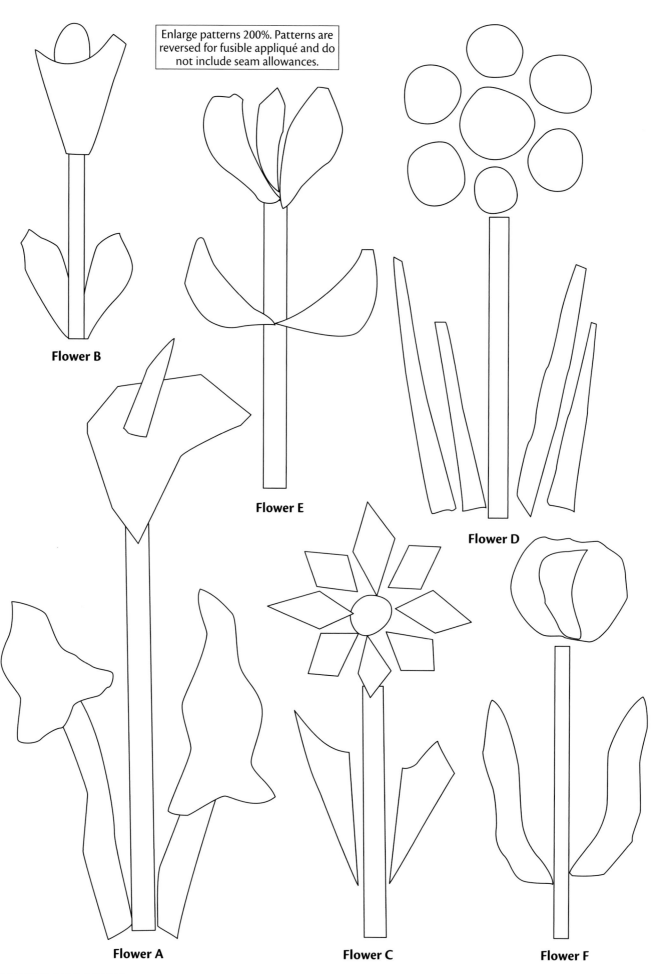

Enlarge patterns 200%. Patterns are reversed for fusible appliqué and do not include seam allowances.

Flower B

Flower E

Flower D

Flower A

Flower C

Flower F

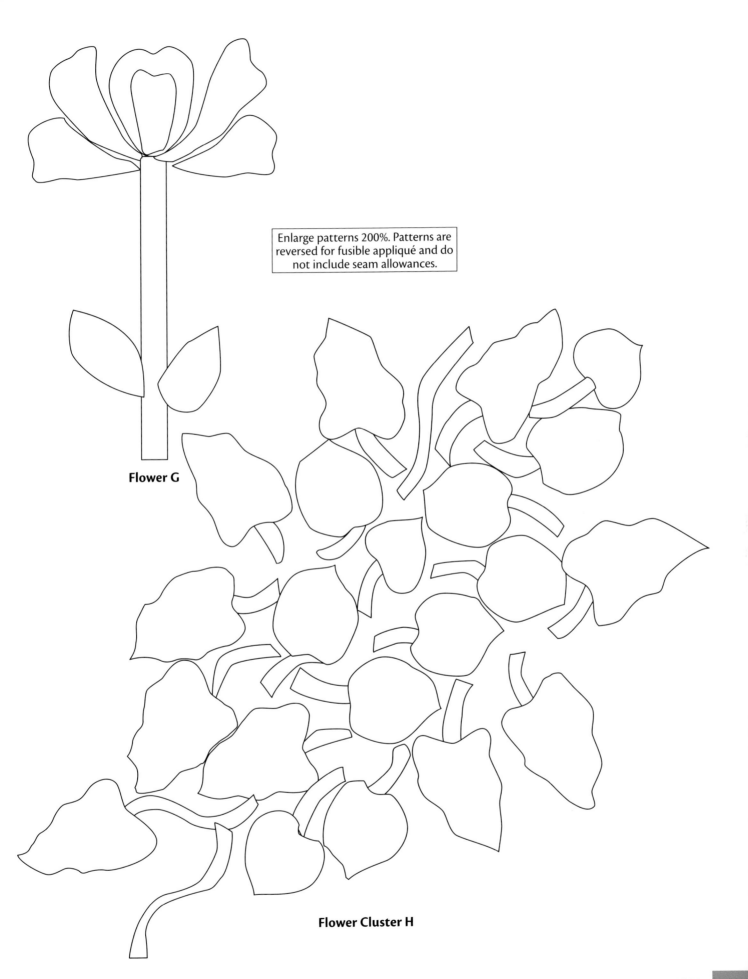

Enlarge patterns 200%. Patterns are reversed for fusible appliqué and do not include seam allowances.

Flower G

Flower Cluster H

FLOWERS and Fronds

True to her style, Jane Sassaman has designed this graphic table runner with intense colors, organic shapes, and controlled wildness. While the borders may seem pieced to the quilt center, the quilt is constructed entirely with fusible appliqué. A one-piece silhouette of leafy shapes unifies and bonds the frame and inner background. A sprinkling of appliquéd posies enlivens the composition with color, texture, and whimsical fun.

As an art quilter, Jane is all about encouraging quilters to depart from her original design. While she used the exciting prints she designed for FreeSpirit, she suggests choosing the fabrics you like to work with. *"The key,"* she explains, *"is to match your silhouette fabric with the background color of your frame, and to choose a subtler or less busy fabric for your background."* Customize the design even further: adjust the length of your runner by adding or subtracting the number of silhouette repeats or consider a cutwork silhouette of your own simple shapes.

By Jane Sassaman

Finished measurements: 18¼" x 65½"

MATERIALS

Yardages are based on fabrics that measure 42" wide. Fat quarters measure 18" x 21".

- 2 yards of multicolored large-scale floral print with black background for outer frame

- 1⅞ yards of light tone-on-tone print for background

- 1⅞ yards of black solid for silhouette and binding

- Fat quarter *each* of dark red, medium red, orange, rust, and blue hand-dyed fabrics for flower appliqués

- 2 yards of fabric for backing

- 22" x 69" piece of batting

- 4 yards of 18"-wide, medium-weight fusible interfacing, such as Pellon ShirTailor Tailoring Fusible

- 2 yards of 18"-wide paper-backed fusible web

- Black, red, orange, yellow, blue, and green machine embroidery thread for appliqué and machine quilting

- Black topstitching thread (12-weight) for machine quilting

- Chalk pencil

- Freezer paper

- Craft knife, such as XACTO, with #11 blade (optional)

CUTTING

For this quilt, cut all strips on the lengthwise grain *of the fabric (parallel to the selvage) unless instructed otherwise.*

From the black solid, cut:

1 piece, 14" x 62"

3 strips, 2½" x 67"

From the backing fabric, cut:

1 piece, 22" x 69"

For Ease and Efficiency

Set up two large tables to work on. Outfit one with a mat and use it as a drawing-and-cutting station. Protect the other with a few layers of fabric to use as an ironing station. Your work will be easier to manage and will stay flat and true.

MAKING THE OUTER FRAME

1. Mark an 18¾" x 66" rectangle onto the smooth side of the interfacing. Rotary cut the rectangle along the marked lines.

2. Position the rectangle of fusible interfacing, fusible side down, on the wrong side of the floral print. Make sure that the selvage edge of the fabric extends at least ¼" beyond the edge of the interfacing and that any regularly repeating motifs on the fabric are spaced evenly along the interfacing edges. Following the manufacturer's instructions, fuse the interfacing to the fabric. Use a rotary cutter to trim ¼" from all edges, leaving an 18¼" x 65½" rectangle as interfaced fabric.

3. Use a sharp chalk pencil in a contrasting color to mark a rectangle 4" from the outside edges of the interfaced fabric. Use a craft knife, a long acrylic ruler, and a cutting mat to cut out the inside rectangle along the marked lines. Set this frame aside, keeping it flat while you work on the next steps.

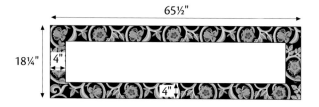

MAKING THE BACKGROUND

1. Use the inner rectangle you cut away (not the frame) as a pattern to trace another rectangle on the smooth side of the remaining interfacing. Cut out the rectangle ¼" outside the traced line.

2. Place the rectangle of interfacing you cut in step 1 on the wrong side of the tone-on-tone print. Make sure that the fabric grain is parallel with the edges of the interfacing, and ¼" from the selvage edges. Fuse the interfacing in place, and then rotary cut directly on the traced line. Place the frame and background pieces right side down on the ironing surface, nesting the background inside the frame. Be sure that they fit together without overlapping; trim if necessary to achieve a perfect fit.

3. Cut 16 "band-aid" strips, 1" x 6", from the remaining interfacing. Center one 1" x 6" strip lengthwise, fusible side down, over each short end where the frame and background edges butt together; fuse in place. Space seven strips evenly along each long edge; fuse. Set this piece aside, keeping it flat.

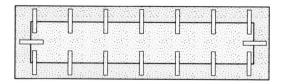

MAKING THE SILHOUETTE

1. Enlarge the frond pattern on page 77 as directed and copy it onto an 11" x 17" sheet of copy paper. Include all dotted and dashed lines. Using a pressing cloth, iron freezer paper to the wrong side of the pattern for added stability. Carefully cut out the yellow shaded areas directly on the marked lines. The remaining white areas will be your pattern.

2. Tape the fusible web, paper side up, to a large, flat surface. Starting ¼" from one long edge, and using large acrylic rulers and a sharp pencil, draw a rectangle, 10¾" x 58". Draw another, smaller rectangle ½" inside the edges of the large rectangle. Place the enlarged pattern from step 1 on the smaller rectangle, aligning the dotted line on the pattern with the top short end of the inner rectangle. Trace the frond, spiraling leaf, and the indications for repeat placement, shown with dashed lines on the pattern.

3. Flip the pattern over to reverse it, align the frond tips and the solid lines along the sides, and trace the mirror image. Continue flipping the pattern and tracing until you have marked the entire silhouette as shown.

Full silhouette layout

4. Working on a large ironing surface, center the fusible web with the traced pattern, fusible side down, on the wrong side of the 14" x 62" piece of black fabric. Pin in the areas between the fronds and spiraling leafs. Follow the manufacturer's instructions for the fusible web, and beginning at the center of the design, press outward in all directions to fuse the web to the fabric wherever there is a frond, spiraling leaf, or area of the rectangular border. Remove pins as you come to them.

5. Working over a cutting mat, rotary cut the outer edges of the rectangle directly on the traced lines. Use a craft knife to cut out the inner silhouette, also on the traced lines. (Embroidery scissors are an alternative, although they tend to be less precise for these graceful curves.) Remove the paper backing. Slide a long sheet of freezer paper underneath the silhouette, and place another piece on top. Secure the layers with a few pins so you can transport and flip the silhouette easily.

6. Place the background and frame right side up on the ironing surface. Place the silhouette on top, fusible side down. Unpin and carefully remove the freezer-paper sheets. Referring to the quilt photo on page 73, position the silhouette over the butted edges of the frame and background so that the join is covered and the silhouette rectangle is straight, with corners square. Use a long acrylic ruler with a right angle to help you line things up; pin and then fuse the silhouette in place.

7. Use black embroidery thread and a fine, medium-width zigzag stitch or satin stitch to secure all cut edges of the silhouette.

MAKING THE APPLIQUÉD FLOWERS

1. Use the patterns on page 76 to make templates for the large and small flowers. Use the templates to trace five large flowers and eight small flowers onto the smooth side of the remaining interfacing. Cut out the shapes directly on the traced lines.

2. Fuse four small flowers to the wrong side of the medium red fabric; repeat using the dark red fabric. Cut out the shapes directly on the traced lines. Use the same method to fuse and cut five large flowers from the orange fabric. Cut out the centers of all flowers as marked.

3. Fuse interfacing to the wrong side of the blue fabric. With right sides facing up, layer a small medium red flower on top of the blue fabric and straight stitch around the raw edge of the flower center to secure the layers. Use orange embroidery thread and a satin stitch to finish the raw edges as shown. Fasten off the thread ends as described in the tip box ("Threads Incognito!") above. Working from the wrong side, trim away the blue fabric ¼" beyond the satin stitching. Repeat to make a total of four small medium red flowers.

Right side of
flower after
stitching

Wrong side of
flower after
trimming

4. Use the method described in step 3 to make four additional small flowers using the dark red fabric. Make five large orange flowers with rust centers, using blue thread for the satin stitching.

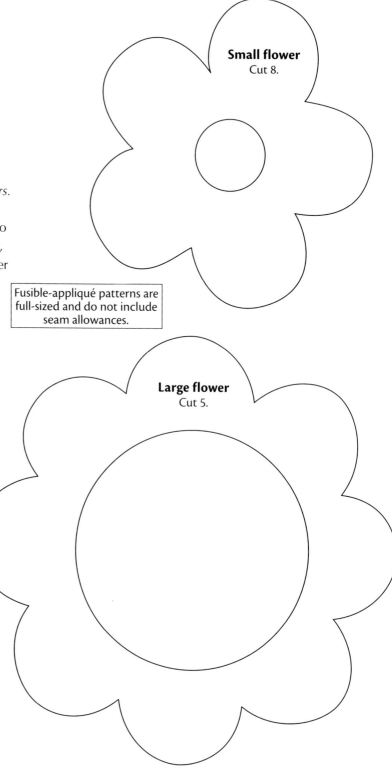

Make a total of eight small flowers and five large flowers.

5. Spread the quilt top out smooth and flat. Referring to the quilt photo on page 73 for suggested placement, pin on the large and small flowers. Baste each flower around its outer edge with matching thread, and then use the same thread to satin stitch over the outer edges.

6. Carefully cut away the background fabric behind each flower center to reduce bulk.

FINISHING

Refer to "Quiltmaking Basics" on page 87 as needed.

1. Press and block your quilt top so it is as straight and square as possible. Trim, if necessary, to measure 18¼" x 65½". Layer the backing, batting, and quilt top; baste.

2. Quilt as desired or as follows: machine quilt using topstitching thread and a matching 50-weight thread in the bobbin. Stitch in the ditch around the outside edge of the silhouette frame with black thread, around the inside of the silhouette with green thread, and around the flowers with red thread. Use red thread to echo quilt approximately ¹/₁₆" outside the flowers and blue thread to echo quilt around the outside of the satin-stitched flower centers. Use yellow thread and a wide satin stitch to add random dashes to the the flower centers. Finish by quilting wavy lines over the entire quilt with black thread.

3. Trim the batting and backing even with the edges of the quilt top. Use the 2½"-wide black strips to make and attach a double-fold binding.

Small flower
Cut 8.

Fusible-appliqué patterns are full-sized and do not include seam allowances.

Large flower
Cut 5.

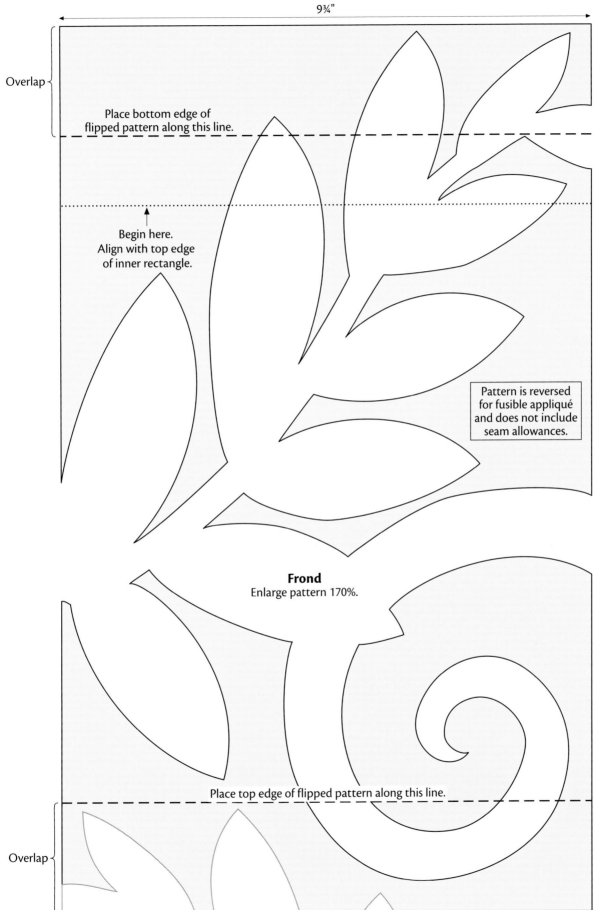

9¾"

Overlap

Place bottom edge of flipped pattern along this line.

Begin here.
Align with top edge
of inner rectangle.

Pattern is reversed
for fusible appliqué
and does not include
seam allowances.

Frond
Enlarge pattern 170%.

Place top edge of flipped pattern along this line.

Overlap

Table LEAF

What dining-room table couldn't use an extra leaf? This leaf won't extend your table's size, but it will extend its style and seasonality! This project, designed by yours truly, the editor, couldn't be easier or more fun to make. An extra layer of felt in the same color as the back sits in for batting and provides a crisp, flat look. The leaf pieces are quick-fused, and the background, the central vein, plus the combination filler and backing are nonwoven felt—so no edges to finish! Easy quilting suggests tributaries of veins running across the leaf, and whirly curlicues flatten and texturize the surface. Make one in every color combo you love, so your table—or walls—can turn over a new leaf each season of the year.

By Eleanor Levie

Finished measurements: 16" x 59"

MATERIALS

Yardages are based on fabric that measures 42" wide unless noted otherwise. Prewash all fabrics, including wool felt, in hot water, to preshrink them and ensure that the colors won't run.

1¾ yards of 36"-wide heathery sage green wool-blend felt for background*

1 yard of 72"-wide black acrylic felt for leaf-stem appliqué, border, and backing

³⁄₈ yard each of purple and rust cotton shot fabrics for leaf appliqués**

6 yards of 18"-wide paper-backed fusible web

Freezer paper

Black 40-weight thread for topstitching

60-weight thread for the bobbin

Pinking shears

Spray mister

This gives you enough for two runners. (See "Resources" on page 91.)
**Shot cottons are from Kaffe Fassett. (See "Resources.")*

CUTTING

From the *length* of the heathery sage green wool felt, cut:
1 piece, 18" x 54"

From the black felt, cut:
1 piece, 16" x 59" (set aside for backing)

PREPARING THE PIECES

Refer to "Fusible Appliqué the Easy Way" on page 88 as needed.

1. Follow the manufacturer's instructions for the fusible web and using a pressing cloth, apply fusible web to the 18" x 54" piece of sage wool felt, the remaining piece of black felt, and the purple and rust cotton fabrics. The fabrics are the same on both sides, so it doesn't matter which side you choose! Leave the paper backing in place.

2. Enlarge and trace the patterns on page 81 to make freezer-paper templates for the leaf pieces (A and B) and the leaf stem (C). Cut out the shapes directly on the traced lines. With waxy sides down, place template A on the right side—that is, the side without the fusible web—of the purple cotton; template B on the right side of the rust cotton; and template C on the right side of the black felt piece you prepared in step 1. Press lightly to hold the freezer paper in place.

3. Use a rotary cutter or scissors to cut out fabric pieces A, B, and C.

ASSEMBLING THE QUILT

1. Carefully remove the paper backing from piece A—in one piece if possible. Repeat for piece B. Retain this paper, called release paper, for marking quilting designs.

2. Spread out the 18" x 54" piece of sage wool felt, paper side down, on a large ironing surface. Referring to the quilt photo on page 79 for guidance as needed, arrange the leaf pieces (A and B) fusible side down on the wool felt, leaving a space between them a bit wider than the leaf stem (C). Remove the release paper from the leaf stem and place it between the leaf pieces, so that a narrow margin of wool felt remains visible.

3. Use a spray mister filled with water to lightly mist the fabrics. Using a pressing cloth, fuse-tack (see the tip box "No Pins! No Thread!" on page 58) and then securely fuse all the leaf pieces in place.

4. Referring again to the quilt photo, use a rotary cutter or scissors to trim the sage wool felt background, leaving a ½" margin around the leaf tip and sides of the stem, and rounding the edge around the base of the stem. Use a rotary cutter and ruler to trim the remaining long sides of the wool felt so the width measures 14". Leaving the leaf tip and stem to extend at either end, square the corners of the wool felt so the long straight sides measure 44" long.

5. Cut a 16" x 59" piece from the remaining fused black felt. Place the piece paper side down on a large ironing surface and center the unit from step 4 on top. Mist the fabrics; using a pressing cloth, fuse-tack and then securely fuse the piece in place.

6. If necessary, use a rotary cutter and ruler to trim the black felt 2" beyond the leaf tip at one end and 4" beyond the rounded stem at the other.

FINISHING

Refer to "Quiltmaking Basics" on page 87 as needed.

1. Use 40-weight black thread in the needle to topstitch the edges of the leaf sections and the leaf stem.

2. Referring to the quilt photo, pencil veins on the dull side of the release paper you removed from the fusible web on fabric pieces A and B. Pin the paper over their coordinating leaf pieces on the quilt. Use a darning foot and follow the penciled lines to free-motion stitch veins along each side of the leaf, backtracking to strengthen the line, and moving along to the next vein without stopping and cutting the thread.

3. Free-motion stitch curlicues along the wool felt background areas.

Topstitching secures each piece; free-motion stitching enhances the background.

4. Remove the paper backing from the black felt. Layer on the 16" x 59" pieced of unprepared felt and fuse to secure. Trim the edges of the bottom layer even with the top layer.

5. Topstitch the outside edges of the sage wool felt, and then topstitch ½" from the edges of the black felt.

6. Use pinking shears to cut all around the quilt, ¼" from the edges.

Hold That Iron!

Wash and dry the quilt, but don't iron it. The wool felt will have a wonderful sherpa-fleece texture.

Enlarge patterns 400%.
Fusible-appliqué patterns do not include seam allowances and are oriented for fusing with Eleanor's technique.

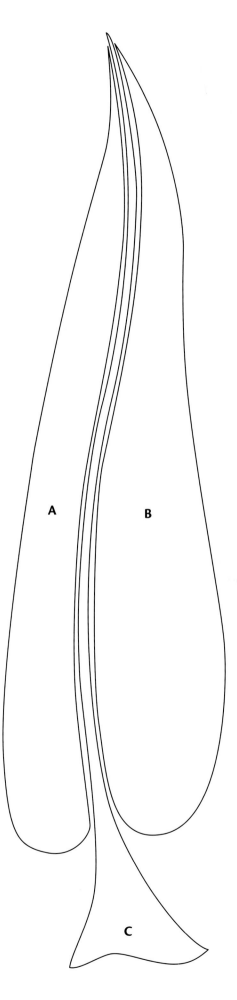

To Diana—
Carol Taylor
5/15/08

Arc-i-TEXTURE

Are you ready to spiral off on an exciting adventure in quiltmaking? Carol Taylor is an art quilter who has made more than 50 small squares in her Arc-i-Texture series. The "Arc" refers to circular couching—which looks a lot harder than it is! "Texture" means combining wildly different types of fabrics with your quilter's cottons. This is your big opportunity to ferret out pieces of fancy fabrics usually lavished on cocktail, bridal, and prom fashions. Dig into your stash and the rummage bins at fabric shops; put those upholstery samples to good use. Carol's Skinny Quilt, which looks smashing both horizontally and vertically, is composed of four square blocks, each one a fused collage in a different value of fabric scraps, from light to dark. A fabric junkie, Carol predicts that *"you, too, will become addicted to making these blocks!"*

By Carol Taylor

Finished measurements: 14½" x 56½"

MATERIALS

Yardages are based on fabrics that measure 42" wide.

1⅞ yards of cotton fabric for backing, facings, and hanging sleeve

1 yard of muslin for foundations*

Scraps or small pieces of at least 30 different fabrics in 3 or 4 colors, each color in values ranging from light to dark, for collaged blocks**

18" x 60" piece of cotton or wool batting

3 yards of 18"-wide fusible web

Pressing cloth or non-stick pressing sheet

Clear monofilament and/or metallic thread for couching

Lightweight thread to match the backing fabric

1 small skein of cotton yarn *or* cording, ⅛" in diameter, in colors to coordinate with fabrics, or 1 large or 2 small skeins of variegated chenille yarn for couching

20 yards of ⅛"-wide variegated, braided ribbon trim (see "Resources" on page 91), or variegated knitting yarn for couched spirals

Cording foot with a large slot, appliqué foot, or walking foot for couching

Basting spray (optional)

Prewash this fabric to remove sizing.

**Choose a wide variety of fibers (cotton, rayon, silk, linen, polyester, velvet and velveteen, organdy and organza, chiffon, and lamé); textures (smooth, sheer, shiny, sueded, embroidered, woven, nappy, low-pile); and prints in various styles and scales.*

CUTTING

Cut all strips on the crosswise grain of the fabric (selvage to selvage) unless instructed otherwise.

From the prewashed muslin, cut:
2 strips, 15" x 42"; crosscut into 4 squares, 15" x 15"

From the *lengthwise grain* of the 1⅞ yards of cotton fabric, cut:
1 rectangle, 18" x 60"
2 strips, 3" x 57"
2 strips, 3" x 15½"

PREPARING THE FABRICS

Refer to "Fusible Appliqué the Easy Way" on page 88 as needed. For these and all the following steps, use a pressing cloth or nonstick pressing sheet to protect your ironing surface and your iron, especially when working with sheer fabrics.

1. Follow the manufacturer's instructions to apply fusible web to all the fabrics except the muslin and backing fabric. When the adhesive has cooled, remove the paper backing from each fabric.

2. Sort the prepared fabrics by value into four stacks: lights, medium-lights, medium-darks, and darks.

MAKING THE BLOCKS

1. Place one 15" muslin square on your ironing surface, and use the various small pieces of prepared fabrics from the lightest stack to compose a collage. Cut three different-sized squares or rectangles from your favorite fabric in that stack so that particular fabric will feature prominently in your piece. Arrange these pieces on the muslin square, spacing them in a way that looks balanced, and keeping all edges parallel and perpendicular to the muslin edges.

2. Choosing from the same stack of light-colored fabrics, cut squares, rectangles, or strips in different sizes. In addition to the size, vary the shapes, colors, and patterns of the pieces. Place the pieces on the muslin square, keeping all edges parallel or perpendicular, and butting or slightly overlapping adjacent pieces. Avoid rigidly aligned rows; offset or stagger the pieces for more visual interest.

3. Position block 1 oriented as it will appear in the finished quilt. Cut larger-than-usual pieces in three different shapes from three of the darker fabrics in the lightest pile to serve as transition pieces. Place a portion of each piece along the bottom (if your quilt will be vertical) or right edge (if your quilt will be horizontal) of block 1, overhanging the edges.

Use three fabrics to create transitions from one block to the next.

4. Place another 15" muslin square directly below block 1 (or to its right, if your design is horizontal). Use scissors to divide the overhanging pieces at the point where the two squares meet, and pin them in place on both blocks. Set block 2 aside.

5. Keeping the transition pieces pinned in place, add or move any other pieces on block 1 until you are satisfied with the composition. Use a hot steam iron to fuse everything in place, removing any pins as you go. Turn the square over and steam-press from the wrong side to ensure that the fusible web is melted completely and that the fabrics are well-bonded. Trim any excess fabric beyond the edges of the muslin.

6. Fuse the three transition pieces to block 2 to ensure a smooth flow from block to block in your finished piece. Then, using the same method you used for block 1, cover the rest of the muslin square with

rectangles, squares, and strips of fabric from the medium-light stack. Position the block beside block 1 as it will appear in the finished quilt, and add three shapes as before to make a transition to block 3.

7. Use the medium-dark stack of fabrics and a 15" muslin square to make block 3 and the dark stack of fabrics and a 15" muslin square to make block 4 in the same way, making sure to include transition pieces between the blocks.

8. Place the four finished blocks on a design wall from lightest to darkest, in either a vertical or horizontal row as you intend for the finished quilt. Stand back so you can better judge whether the colors and values flow nicely. Add additional fabric pieces to improve the flow if needed.

Making Changes

If a single fabric piece calls too much attention to itself, try toning it down by partially covering it with another fabric. If you want to remove any fused piece entirely, heat it with an iron to melt the glue, pull the piece off, and then fuse another piece in its place.

ASSEMBLING THE QUILT

1. When you are happy with the balance and flow of the fabrics, use a 1/2" seam to sew the blocks together. Press the seam allowances open.

2. Layer the backing, batting, and quilt top; baste. You can use a spray adhesive to secure the layers or use your preferred method of basting.

COUCHING

As you couch, you will be simultaneously quilting your quilt. For a subtle finish, match the yarns to the color or tone of the adjacent fabrics.

1. Outfit your machine with a cording foot, threading the yarn or cording through the slot. (If you don't have a cording foot, use an appliqué foot or walking foot and guide the yarn with your hands.) Use clear monofilament or lightweight metallic thread on top and a lightweight cotton thread that matches the backing in the bobbin. Set the stitch width so the needle swings just

wide enough to cover the ribbon or yarn. Set a long stitch length to show off the ribbon or yarn and keep the thread from being noticeable.

Practice, Practice

Before you stitch, practice couching on a sandwich of scrap fabrics and batting in order to test and adjust the tension as well as the length and width of your stitches.

2. Begin along an edge of the quilt top, and position the yarn over any nearby raw edges. Sew a few tiny straight stitches forward and back to back-tack, and then sew long zigzag stitches over the yarn.

3. Cover all raw edges that match or coordinate with that particular yarn. Turn corners where appropriate, and keep a continuous line of yarn for as long as possible, although it's fine to backtrack for a short distance to continue without cutting the yarn. When you do need to end a line or change yarn colors, back-tack and clip the yarn and threads at those points, close to the surface. Couch with one color throughout, and then go on to another. Continue until you have covered all the raw edges except for the perimeter of the quilt top.

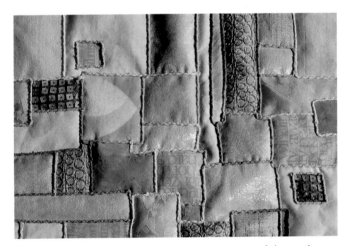

Couch all raw edges except for the perimeter of the quilt top.

4. Next, couch variegated braided ribbon or yarn thread for the spirals. Begin near the center of the quilt, and bring the bobbin thread up to the top. Leaving a 1" tail, secure the yarn to the quilt with a few tiny back-tack stitches. Set the zigzag width to span the width of the yarn, and set the stitch length as long as possible.

5. Take one stitch, lift the presser foot to turn, rotate your work a quarter turn, take another stitch, and lift the presser foot to turn again. Continue one stitch at a time to get a tight center for your spiral.

6. When you make it around to where you took your first stitch, clip the loose ends of the yarn and threads where you started. Using the edge of your presser foot as a guide, take two stitches and lift the presser foot and make a quarter turn. Be sure to keep the edge of the presser foot right alongside the yarn as you turn. Slowly spiral around and outward, using the presser foot to maintain a uniform distance and curve.

7. As your circle gets wider, you can take more stitches before stopping to pivot. Once you're beyond the first two to three rounds, the stitching will become much quicker and easier. Make some large spirals with about 14 rounds and some smaller ones with about 11 rounds, spacing them randomly on the surface. Overlap the edges of some spirals and make partial spirals along the quilt edges. Finally, fill in any large empty spaces with small spirals of 3 to 7 rounds. View your piece on a design wall to decide if additional spirals are needed, and where and how large they should be.

A couched spiral

FINISHING

Refer to "Quiltmaking Basics" on page 87 as needed.

1. Press and block your quilt so it is as straight and square as possible. Trim the batting and backing even with the edges of the quilt top.

2. Finish the edges of the quilt with facings. With wrong sides together, press each 3"-wide cotton strip in half lengthwise. Place one 57"-long folded strip right sides together with one long side of the quilt top, aligning the raw edges; pin. Sew the strip to the quilt with a ¼" seam. Use a steam iron to press the facing flat, and then wrap the entire strip to the back of the quilt and press to flatten the seam allowance. Slipstitch the folded edge of the facing to the back of the quilt. Repeat to sew, press, and stitch a facing to the opposite long side of the quilt.

3. Center a 15½"-long folded cotton strip on one short end of the quilt, aligning the long raw edges and allowing a ½" overhang at each end; pin. Sew the strip to the quilt with a ¼" seam. Fold the ends of the facing strip under, turn the facing to the back of the quilt, and slipstitch the folded edge of the facing to the back of the quilt. Repeat to sew, press, and stitch a facing to the opposite sort side of the quilt.

4. Use the remaining backing fabric to make a hanging sleeve.

Get the skinny here on general techniques! Beginners: read through this section before you begin a project. Experienced quilters: refer to this info on an "as-needed" basis.

JUST BETWEEN US MATERIAL GIRLS AND GUYS

Yardage amounts for quilter's cottons are based on 42" widths unless otherwise indicated. When possible, the project instructions suggest fat quarters (18" x 21") or fat eighths (9" x 21"). Prewash all cotton fabrics with hot water, and dry in the dryer to preshrink them—loosely woven fabrics, such as flannel, will shrink a lot—and to remove excess dyes. Always remove the selvages—the ¼" of tightly woven fabric along the lengthwise edges of the yardage.

DON'T WANT NO FAT BATTS HERE

A Skinny Quilt shouldn't be puffy, especially if it will be used on a table. Choose your favorite thin batting, or splurge on something special—after all, you don't need a lot! Fusible fleece makes sandwiching your quilt a cinch. Art quilters such as Carol Taylor and Yvonne Porcella swear by wool batting. As an alternative, forgo batting altogether and consider flannel, interfacing, or felt for a filler.

SUPPLIES, SUPPLIES!

Here's what you'll want to have handy:

- Paper, tracing paper, and freezer paper, for patterns
- Rotary-cutting supplies (see "Cut to the Chase" at right).
- Sewing machine in good working order
- Thread snips or small embroidery scissors
- Pins, especially flat flower pins, so you can place a rotary ruler on top
- Pincushion
- Fabric markers for light and dark fabrics. (Always test on your fabrics before you use them to be sure the marks will come out.)

- Seam ripper for those inevitable "oops" moments, and tweezers for pulling out threads
- Steam iron, ironing surface, and nonstick pressing sheet (See "Pressing Issues" on page 88.)

The specific project instructions list any additional supplies you'll need for that project.

CUT TO THE CHASE

Most projects in this book involve rotary cutting, and require a cutter with a sharp 45 mm blade, a cutting mat, and acrylic rulers. For your cutting mat, the larger the better, and two or even three 24" x 36" mats placed end to end are great, especially for squaring up your quilt before the binding is added.

As to rulers, a 15" square and a 6" x 24" rectangle will be invaluable for cutting backgrounds, borders, and backings, as well as for squaring up accurately. This is especially crucial if the Skinny Quilt will hang vertically on a wall, but you'll also want the edges of your table runner to run parallel to the table.

AN IMPORTANT MESSAGE FROM THE BORDERS

Border measurements are provided as a guide only. Your quilt may end up a little taller or shorter, fatter or skinnier than the dimensions indicate, depending on your seam allowances, cutting, and pressing techniques. Hey, this is a Skinny Quilt, after all, and it's rare that it must be an exact size. However, you don't want to deal with precut borders that are too small for the finished quilt top. So, if you can, wait and measure the quilt top before cutting borders to the *exact lengths* you need.

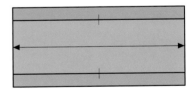

Measure the longest dimension through the center. Mark centers.

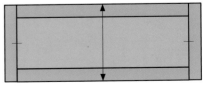

Measure the shortest dimension through the center, including border strips. Mark centers.

PIECE AND HARMONY

Unless otherwise indicated, place pieces together with right sides facing and edges even. Insert pins at the corners first, at seams that must match, and at intervals in between. Take care to remove pins as your machine needle reaches them; stitching over them will often break the needle. Machine stitch leaving ¼" seam allowances.

PRESSING ISSUES

For piecing, you can often finger-press seams until you finish a unit, make multiple units, and then do all pressing with an iron. Use a hot, dry setting for cotton, or the setting appropriate for the most temperamental fabric you are using. Never iron directly on metallics, synthetics, or fancy fabrics; use a nonstick pressing cloth as a "go-between."

FUSIBLE APPLIQUÉ THE EASY WAY

Before applying fusible web to fabrics, wash the fabrics to remove any sizing or finishes. Don't use fabric softener, as that will keep you from getting a good bond.

Follow the manufacturer's instructions for the fusible product you are using; in general, you will be directed to place fusible web rough side down on the wrong side of your fabric. (Use a pressing cloth, nonstick pressing sheet, or piece of release paper to protect the iron and ironing surface.) Place a hot iron on the fabric for several seconds. Repeat across the surface so that every area of the fabric gets fused.

Cut out fused fabrics with sharp blades—either a rotary cutter or fabric shears. Use small, sharp scissors to cut curvy or small shapes and inset corners. Pin or fuse-tack (see the tip box "No Pins! No Thread!" on page 58) the pieces in place.

When you are ready to secure everything permanently, go to town with the fusing: Set the glue by pressing the quilt top for 10 seconds, using a steam iron or, if you prefer, a damp pressing cloth. Your iron must be consistently hot; use the cotton setting. Such pressing will provide a good bond between the fabrics and flattens the quilt. Steam-press from the back as well.

REV YOUR ENGINES: MACHINE APPLIQUÉ AHEAD

For appliqué or topstitching, use a heavier thread in the needle, such as a 40-weight rayon or cotton. Test your machine's tension, as the fused fabric and background are a firmer surface than usual. Fused appliqués are less prone to ravel, but need at least topstitching to ensure they don't eventually lift. To cover the edges, use decorative stitching. Satin-stitching (that is, a fine zigzag stitch), the blanket stitch, and the buttonhole stitch are all good options. If your machine has other decorative stitches, give 'em a whirl.

MAKING A SANDWICH

Cut batting and backing fabric 2" larger all around than the quilt top. For sandwiching the layers, basting spray can be a quilter's best friend. Place the backing right side down on a large, flat surface, and spray. Smooth the batting on top. Spray again. Center the quilt top right side up over the batting and backing. As an alternative to spraying, use safety pins or giant basting stitches to secure the layers and keep them from shifting.

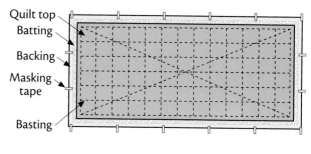

Quilt top
Batting
Backing
Masking tape
Basting

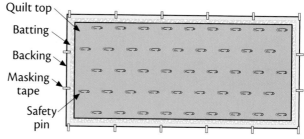

Quilt top
Batting
Backing
Masking tape
Safety pin

QUILT WITHOUT GUILT

In a rush to finish? Stitch in the ditch—that is, right along the seams—with a walking foot, to anchor key seams and stitch around the major elements of your Skinny Quilt. Care to add more pattern and color? Do it with an open-toed embroidery foot, and use any decorative machine stitches your machine offers. Cover raw edges with couching (page 85) or satin stitching that quilts simultaneously.

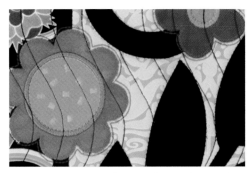

Simple satin stitching and wavy lines of straight stitches

For free-motion quilting, some quilters prefer to lower, or at least cover, the feed dogs on their machine. But the key to this popular technique is a darning foot, which allows you to move the quilt sandwich in any direction. The trick, unless you have a new sewing machine with a stitch regulator, is getting stitches that are consistent in length. The rate at which you move the piece and run the machine must be smooth, consistent, and compatible. This takes a lot of practice, so experiment on a test piece that is similar in thickness to your project until you are comfortable with the technique.

Shown here are three common free-motion patterns that fill space nicely.

Meander stitch

Loop-de-loop

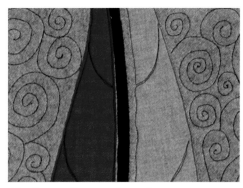

Curlicues. Start each curlicue at its center, making a few stitches in place before spiraling out.

After quilting, trim the long edges and then the short edges of your Skinny Quilt. Use the ruler and the grid on the cutting mat to keep your piece square. Block your Skinny Quilt by spraying it with water and pinning it to a large ironing surface to gently stretch the edges as needed. Steam-press, or let the piece dry thoroughly. Wait 24 hours, and unpin.

PLAYING HANGMAN—OR HANG WOMAN

If your Skinny Quilt will hang on a wall, you'll want to make a sleeve or casing for a rod. Cut a rectangle of fabric 3" shorter than the top edge of the quilt by 4½" wide. Hem the short ends of the rectangle, fold it lengthwise in half, and lightly press. Center it along the top edge of the backing, with raw edges even. As you bind your quilt, these raw edges will be enclosed. Slipstitch along the bottom fold of the casing to secure it to the backing. For a Skinny Quilt that hangs flat, do as Yvonne Porcella does and include a narrower rod pocket at the bottom to encase a 1"-wide aluminum slat.

The easiest way to bind your quilt is with a double-fold binding, a separate strip for each side of your quilt. If you prefer to have mitered corners, start with joined binding several inches longer than the distance all around your quilt.

1. Cut strips in the widths given in the project instructions and then piece the strips with diagonal seams that are pressed open as shown.

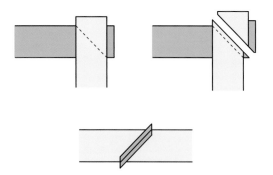

2. Trim the starting end of the binding strip at a 45° angle and fold it under to make a small hem. Fold the binding strips in half lengthwise, wrong sides together, and press.

3. Start at the bottom of the quilt, a few inches from a corner, and leaving a 5" tail. With raw edges aligned, pin the binding to the quilt. Use a ¼" seam to stitch the binding to the quilt, removing pins as you come to them.

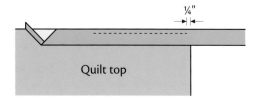

4. To miter the corners, stop stitching ¼" from a corner, and take a backstitch. Remove the quilt from under the presser foot, and fold the binding up so it's flush with the adjacent edge. Fold the binding down again,

alongside the new edge. Insert the needle ¼" from both sides, take a couple of stitches, and backstitch.

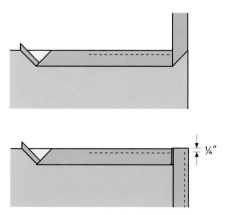

5. When you approach the place where you began, overlap the folded starting end, and trim the finishing end of the binding at a 45° angle. Finish sewing the binding to the quilt.

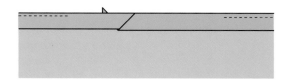

6. Bring the folded edge of the binding over the edges of the quilt sandwich, and pin it to the backing. Use thread in a color that matches the binding and slip-stitch along the fold to cover the machine stitching.

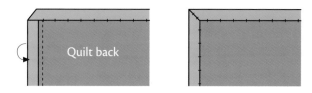

Save a Step

Try this super-easy, super-quick binding technique from Terry Atkinson. Stitch the double-fold binding to the right side of the quilt as usual, and pin it to the back, at least ⅛" beyond the stitching. On the front, stitch in the ditch along the binding, which simultaneously topstitches the binding on the back.

AT THE FINISH LINE

Once the quilt is done, you may need to rinse out any spray starch or any markings you made in cutting, tracing, or quilting.

Don't stop until you've added a label to the back of the quilt. Sign and date your work, and consider writing a personal message for the recipient or documenting the occasion for which you made it. Create text and clip art on the computer, and print it all out onto prepared fabric sheets for photo-transfer. Or, use a fine-tip permanent fabric marker and heat-set the lettering. Either fuse the label to the back, or turn the edges under and slip-stitch them in place, penetrating the backing only. If you would like to quilt your label, stitch it by hand, going just through the backing and batting but not through to the quilt top.

Hooray! Your Skinny Quilt is all done!

RESOURCES

Barb Cribb's fabric packs for "A Garden of Seasons," or wool in bundles, yardage:
Wild Thymes Pattern Company
www.wildthymespatternco.com

Beads for "A Garden of Seasons":
Beyond Beadery
www.beyondbeadery.com

Dupioni silk, batiste, and taffeta for "Arnold Marathon," "Arc-i-Texture," or other Skinny Quilts:
www.fabric.com
www.denverfabrics.com

Feedsack Lady's fat-quarter bundles of feed-sack-style prints for "Morning Stars":
www.feedsacklady.com
Darlene Zimmerman's fabric collections:
Robert Kaufman
www.robertkaufman.com

Kaffe Fassett fabrics, including prints as used in "Rosy Runner," and shot cottons in Ginger (rust) and Cassis (purple) as used in "Table Leaf":
www.gloriouscolor.com

Laura Wasilowski's hand-dyed cotton, rayon, and silk fabrics; hand-dyed threads and ribbons:
Artfabrik
www.artfabrik.com

Lynne Hagmeier's fabric packs, with fabric similar to those used in "Sunflower Duet":
Kansas Troubles Quilting
www.KTquilts.com
Lynne Hagmeier's fabric collections:
Moda Fabrics
www.moda.com

Templates:
Tri-Recs and Companion Angles from EZ Quilting
www.ezquilt.com
My Favorite Log Cabin Ruler #8037 from Marti Michell
www.frommarti.com

Wonder Invisible Thread, and other decorative and metallic threads:
YLI Corporation
www.ylicorp.com

WoolFelt (wool-rayon blend) and FiestaFelt (acrylic) for "Table Leaf":
National Nonwovens
www.nationalnonwovens.com

Terry Atkinson (www.atkinsondesigns.com) is a former teacher of home ec and adult-ed quilting, as well as a long-time Girl Scout leader. Her first quilt, a Drunkard's Path, is still not completely quilted! Since embarking on that project, she has focused on simple machine-pieced and quilted pieces that cleverly look like they are more work than they really are. She enjoys every part of quilting—except for finishing! With hundreds of quilt patterns to her credit, Terry is the designer and pattern writer for Atkinson Designs, a family-run quilt pattern business in Elk River, Minnesota. Husband Kirk is the business manager, and son Derek and daughter Megan help out wherever they can.

Barb Cribb (www.wildthymespatternco.com) has the first quilt she made when she was still a teenager in 1974, and uses it as a teaching tool when she presents classes to beginners. She has taught quiltmaking for years and her work has been juried into several international shows. Her interest in wool started in 1997 and her Wild Thymes Pattern Co. took off in 1999 like a frisky lamb; she now has more than 50 titles in her line. Her company supplies patterns, kits, classes, hand-dyed wool, and information to the quilt world. Barb, who likes to sign her letters "Wildly sincere," lives in Bozeman, Montana, with husband John and daughter Sunny; two older sons have quite unsheepishly left the fold, or nearly so.

Karen Eckmeier (www.quilted-lizard.com) is an award-winning fiber artist and national teacher, producing patterns and books under the name The Quilted Lizard. A self-described "serious doodler," Karen loves lines, textures, and lizards! She often relies on a spontaneous approach to working with fabric, randomly cutting, layering, and topstitching fabric strips to convey the feeling of a scene. Her unique techniques include "Layered Curves," "Happy Villages," and "Accidental Landscapes." Karen and her husband live in Kent, Connecticut, in their newly built dream house filled with light and quilts.

Lynne Hagmeier

Marti Michell

Kaffe Fassett (right) and **Liza Prior Lucy** (left) (www.gloriouscolor.com) have been working together since 1990, designing quilts and writing books that feature them. Kaffe is a Californian who has made London his home since the 1960s. He is a painter who is best known for his unique sense of color. His books on knitting, needlepoint, and mosaics, as well as patchwork and appliqué, feature lush photographs of Kaffe's colorful work in locations all over the world. Quiltmaker Liza Prior Lucy lives in Pennsylvania and has an online fabric shop that specializes in selling fabric designed by Kaffe for the Rowan Company. Together Kaffe and Liza merge their colorful sensibilities to reinterpret traditional quilt patterns using contemporary fabrics and unexpected color combinations. Separately, more often than not, they travel the world lecturing and teaching about quiltmaking. They are both happiest in their respective studios, cutting fabric, arranging it on design walls, sewing, and singing badly.

(www.ktquilts.com) knows about Kansas Troubles. As a young widow with four small children, Lynne took time off from doing social work and discovered the pleasures of rotary cutting and quiltmaking. Along with two friends, she made little quilts to sell at local craft shows, then began publishing patterns for quilt shops to carry. Now the sole owner and designer of Kansas Troubles Quilters, Lynne has dozens of patterns, books, and fabric designs for Moda to her credit. After the last kid went off to college, she and her husband, Robert, moved to Lynne's childhood hometown of Bennington, Kansas, where they enjoy visits from their seven grandchildren, run retreats for quilters in what was formerly a pool hall, and stock their antiques shop across the street with whimsical collectibles and quilts.

(www.frommarti.com), the Silver Star honoree of 2004 (honor conveyed by Quilts Inc. for her contributions to quilting and textile art), is clearly a pioneer and a major force in the current quilt revival. In 1972 when Marti and her husband, Richard, started Yours Truly, Inc., a patchwork kit company, there was no quilt industry. Since then, she has contributed in almost every capacity. Whether she is participating as a teacher, quilter, author, publisher, manufacturer, designer, consultant, judge, and quilt collector, or promoting talented quilters into prominence, her enthusiasm for quilting is always evident. Since 1995 the Michells have manufactured the From Marti Michell line of acrylic templates and specialty rulers. The former Martha Glenn—a farm girl from Iowa who won many a 4-H club ribbon—is a longtime resident of Atlanta, Georgia.

Linda Pool
(www.lindaslace.com) is a quilt
teacher, lecturer, author, and judge.
Her "Linda's Lace" was the first
quilt that showed her cutwork technique, and it won multiple awards.
She has designed and publishes a
line of cutwork patterns for reverse
appliqué under the heading Very
Victorian, LLC. Linda lives in Vienna,
Virginia, where she is the book-
keeper for her family's Mercedes
repair business, a mother of four,
and a grandmother of (at last count)
three. Her creative expression
extends to singing and dollhouse
miniatures, including a varied
collection of miniature quilts that are
scaled to fit her miniature scenes.

**Yvonne
Porcella**
(www.yvonneporcella.com) started
out as an operating-room nurse and
a weaver. Since the early 1960s,
she's been an innovator who specializes in unique wearables and art
quilts. She both hand paints fabrics
to achieve soft watercolor effects,
and combines bold and vibrant
commercial fabrics for dynamic
masterpieces. Her work is featured
in major exhibitions, art galleries,
and museums. Yvonne is the founder
and past president of the board of
Studio Art Quilt Associates (SAQA).
She is a teacher, author, and recipient of the prestigious Silver Star
Award, conveyed by Quilts Inc. for
her contributions to quilting and
textile art.

Jane Sassaman
(www.janesassaman.com) is a
contemporary quilt artist, fabric
designer, author, and teacher
whose bold designs celebrate the
energy and miraculous beauty of
garden flowers and plants. Her
quilt "Willow" was named one of
the 100 best American quilts of
the twentieth century. Since 2002,
Jane has been designing exuberant
and large-scale prints for FreeSpirit
Fabrics. Drenched in exciting color,
they've been affectionately referred
to as "William Morris on antide-
pressants!" Recently, Jane and her
husband moved from an old house
to a contemporary cottage with
enough personality to complement
and encourage their work. It should
come as no surprise that this home
outside Chicago is surrounded by
fields and forest.

Laurie Shifrin
(laurieshifrin@aol.com) is the author
of two popular quilt books, *Batik
Beauties* and *Batiks and Beyond*,
both published by Martingale &
Company. Originally a professional
violinist living on the East Coast,
Laurie now makes her living as a
professional quilter in the beautiful city of Seattle, Washington. She
is also technical editor for In The
Beginning's quilt publications and
was retail manager of their store
until it closed in 2006. She is a
national teacher traveling around the
country sharing her love of batiks,
her beautiful quilt designs, and her
no-nonsense style of quilting.

Avis Shirer
(www.joinedatthehip.com) designs quilt patterns with her best buddy and business partner, Tammy Johnson, with whom she shares the company—and the feeling of being—Joined at the Hip. They first met while working on a grain elevator, and later staffed a local quilt shop. Together they've authored the book *Alphabet Soup*, had work published and self-published, produced over 1,000 different patterns, and designed prints and woven fabrics for Clothworks. Both women grew up and continue to live in rural northern Iowa, where they host annual retreats for quilters and let the seasons inspire their work.

Carol Taylor
(www.caroltaylorquilts.com) just may be the most prolific quilter of the entire quilt world. Since she began quilting in 1993, she has created nearly 500 masterpieces, from small to quite large. Carol has won six Best of Show awards (with six different quilts!), along with dozens of other major prizes. Vibrant colors, striking contrasts, and exciting machine-quilting designs distinguish her body of work, though her series include very different genres and techniques. "Retired" after 22 years of headhunting—that is to say, running her own recruiting business—she devotes most of her time to teaching workshops nationally and internationally. This often gives her a welcome respite from the cold and snow of life in upstate New York. Nonetheless, Carol always manages to squeeze in time for doting on her young grandsons and exploring ever more amazing challenges in her quiltmaking.

Laura Wasilowski
(www.artfabrik.com) is a self-proclaimed "serial quilter," a contemporary quilt artist, author, teacher, humorist, and creator of colorful hand-dyed fabrics and threads. Her pictorial art quilts often chronicle her life. Each wall piece she makes takes fused appliqué and machine quilting to a loftier place. As the Dean of Corrections for the deliciously fictitious Chicago School of Fusing, Laura claims—with tongue firmly in cheek—to present classes on fusing etiquette and deportment.

Darlene Zimmerman
(www.feedsacklady.com) once went by the moniker "Granny." But it's only recently that she became a grandmother—a youthful one at that—and her color palettes, quilt patterns, books, and kits always have a fresh and lively flair. Now known as the Feedsack Lady, Darlene is a designer who specializes in 1930s fabrics and classics in patchwork and appliqué. She also teaches and designs quilting tools that make quilting easier and more accessible for today's busy quilters. Married, and with four grown children, she is part of a long line of women who sew and quilt. She lives in a small farming community in rural Minnesota, very near the farm where she grew up.

About the EDITOR

Eleanor Levie
(www.eleanorlevie.com) had a happy childhood in Baltimore, Maryland, despite being painfully skinny. Since 1978 she has worked as a needlework and crafts editor, author, and book producer, with quilting as a specialty. Elly is also a quilter herself—one who has had many chances to learn from the experts while she edits their books and chapters! She has a passion for inspiring new and experienced quilters to try new techniques, and to appreciate quilts as art *and* as craft. She presents lectures and workshops on innovative themes and techniques to guilds and museum groups.

Home is Bucks County, Pennsylvania, where she and her DH (darling hubby) both do most of their work from home. While their son is away at college, their nest is not empty; their guard-bird, Spike, whistles and sings to signal that guests are arriving. Because Elly no longer eats like a bird, her skinny days are behind her, and she resorts to such tricks as wearing lots of slimming black and standing around funhouse mirrors that make you look long and lean. *Photo taken at Giggleberry Fair in Peddler's Village, Lahaska, Pennsylvania by Great Circle Photography of Doylestown, Pennsylvania.*